THE CASE
OF THE ALLEGIANCE
DUE TO
SOVERAIGN POWERS

by

WILLIAM SHERLOCK

Published by *The Rota* at the University of Exeter
1979

© The Rota
ISBN : 0 904617 14 9

The Rota is an independent, academic society,
wholly supported by its subscribers.
Its sole purpose is the publication of facsimiles
of the Stuart era.
This is the twenty-fourth pamphlet published by *The Rota*.
For more information please contact
Maurice Goldsmith or Ivan Roots
at the University of Exeter.

Printed in Great Britain by
The Printing Unit of the University of Exeter

PREFATORY NOTE

Among the two hundred tracts put out after the Glorious Revolution debating the legitimacy of the new régime, the most influential and combative was William Sherlock's tory *The case of the allegiance*. Although the title page is dated 1691 *The case* was published on 3 November 1690; a sixth edition was in print by mid-January 1691. Editions were also published at Dublin and Edinburgh. The pamphlet sparked off a major controversy, stimulating more than fifty replies or defences. Sherlock's opponents included whig polemicists like William Atwood and Samuel Johnson, prominent non-jurors such as Jeremy Collier, John Kettlewell, Thomas Wagstaffe and George Hickes, and Grub Street hacks like Tom D'Urfey and Tom Brown. Leibniz and Locke both wrote manuscript commentaries. (Locke's notes — Bodl., MS Locke c. 28, fos. 83-96 — have not yet been published. On Liebniz, see P. Riley, 'An unpublished ms of Leibniz on the allegiance due to sovereign powers', *Journal of the History of Philosophy* 11 (1972), 319-26, and N. Jolley, 'Leibniz on Hobbes, Locke's *Two Treatises* and Sherlock's *Case of Allegiance*', *Historical Journal* 18 (1975), 21-36.)

Sherlock, a popular preacher and controversialist, had already written on the subject in 1684, upholding the tory doctrine of absolute non-resistance in *The case of resistance*. At the Revolution, he became a leading jacobite and a quarrelsome non-juror, arguing against the removal of James. He was suspended from his appointments on 1 August 1689 according to the Act for the new oaths, but resumed preaching on 1 February 1690, praying publicly for William and Mary as king and queen *de facto*. On 20 August he wrote to Sancroft, the ejected primate, asserting that his thoughts were 'all on fire' since a 'sudden revelation' 'choques me'. Soon afterwards he took the oaths. *The case* was Sherlock's apologia.

Among motives alleged for his conversion were the realization of the decisiveness of the battle of the Boyne, his wife's bullying and his own hunger for preferment. (He was reappointed Master of the Temple and in 1691 became Dean of St Paul's.) His own explanation was that reading Canon 28 of Bishop Overall's *Convocation book* (the canons of 1606), published by Sancroft in the non-juror cause, had convinced him that allegiance was owed to a régime that was 'thoroughly settled'. (See his letter to Sancroft, Bodl., Rawlinson D836, fo. 195.)

The doctrine Sherlock expounded was not new and, in fact, was widely used in the Revolution debate. It reiterated the position taken in the Engagement controversy of 1649-50 by such *de facto* theorists as Ascham and Nedham and, indeed, by Hobbes. Theoretical rights of the rival claimants and nice constitutional points were irrelevant to the obligation to obey. All that need be considered was which régime was in plenary possession of the administration. That régime by possessing and protecting the subjects so had God's authority. To it *Romans* 13 commanded obedience. Sherlock insisted that he had not abandoned non-resistance. It was providence which had removed James. But the absence of a social contract and its overtly providentialist rhetoric made the doctrine seem Hobbesian — an implication from which Sherlock attempted to dissociate himself, insisting in a subsequent tract that the duty of submission was demonstrated 'without asserting the principles of Mr Hobbs'.

The pamphlet angered radical whigs because it justified the Revolution without recourse to a social contract or the rights of subjects; it outraged jacobites by its immoral equation of right with might. In the subsequent debate Sherlock was pilloried for apostacy while controversy raged over the meaning of *Romans* 13, Overall's *Convocation book*, the *de jure/de facto* distinction and Sherlock's 'old fanatick way of expounding providence'.

For further discussion see J. P. Kenyon, *Revolution principles* (Cambridge, 1977), pp. 5-34; G. L. Cherry, 'The legal and philosophical position of the jacobites, 1688-89', *Journal of Modern History* 22 (1950), 309-21; Mark Goldie, 'Edmund Bohun and *jus gentium* in the Revolution debate, 1689-1693', *Historical Journal* 20 (1977), 569-86; C. F. Mullett, 'A case of allegiance: William Sherlock and the Revolution of 1688', *Huntington Library Quarterly* 10 (1946-47), 83-103; G. M. Straka, 'The final phase of divine right theory in England, 1688-1702', *English Historical Review* 77 (1962), 638-58. Mark Goldie, to whom *The Rota* is greatly indebted for the substance of this *Note*, will shortly publish 'Political obligation and the Revolution of 1689: an annotated bibliography of pamphlets', *Bulletin of Research in the Humanities* (forthcoming, 1980).

No substantial variations among the London editions have been discovered; the Edinburgh edition is in a different format; the Dublin edition has not been examined. This edition is reprinted with the permission of the British Library from shelf mark 8005. f. 35.; Wing S3269.

THE CASE OF THE ALLEGIANCE DUE TO Soveraign Powers,

STATED and RESOLVED,

According to SCRIPTURE and REASON, AND THE Principles of the *Church of England*,

WITH A more particular Respect to the OATH, lately enjoyned, of Allegiance to Their Present MAJESTIES, K. *WILLIAM* and Q. *MARY*.

By *WILLIAM SHERLOCK*, D. D
Master of the TEMPLE.

LONDON:
Printed for W. Rogers, at the *Sun* over against St. *Dunstans* Church in *Fleet-street*. 1691.

THE
PREFACE.

I Need not acquaint the World with the Occasion of publishing this Book; which indeed is extorted from me by the rude Clamours and unchristian Censures of some, and the earnest Importunities of others.

My taking the Oath of Allegiance to King William and Queen Mary, after so long a Refusal, has occasioned a great deal of talk, and a great many uncharitable guesses about it; Faction and blind Zeal always wanting either the Wit, or the good Will, to guess right.

One would have thought it the most probable Conjecture, That a Man, who had forfeited all his Preferments by refusing the Oath, and had for ever lost them, had not the Government been more mild and gentle in delaying the Execution of the Law, acted very honestly and sincerely in it; and if so, That there is also good Reason to believe, that if the same Person afterwards takes the Oath, he acts honestly in that too: for what Reason is there to suspect, that he, who would not swear against the present persuasion of his Conscience to keep his Preferments, should swear against his Conscience to get them again? I do not know, that I have given any just Occasion to the World to mark me out for a Dishonest Man, or a Fool; I may be mistaken, and so may any Body else, though never so Wise and honest: But this I am sure of, that I never acted

A   with

The PREFACE.

with more sincerity in any Affair of my whole Life, than I have done in this Matter, from the beginning to the end; and whether I have sufficient Reason for what I do, I refer to the trial of this Discourse.

The truth is, though I refused to take the Oaths, I never engaged in any Faction against it: I never made it my Business to disswade Men from it: When my Opinion was asked, I declared my own Thoughts, but I never sought out Men to make Proselytes.

While I thought it an ill thing, I was secretly concerned, that some of my old intimate Friends had taken the Oaths; but yet as Opportunity served, I conversed with those of them, whose Zeal had not made their Conversation uneasie, with the same Friendship and Freedom, that I used to do: I believed them to be honest Men, and that they acted honestly, according to the perswasion of their own Minds, and wished that I could have done as they did. I complied with the Government, as far as I thought I could with a safe Conscience: I always lived quietly and peaceably, and was ready to have given Security to do so. I prayed for King William and Queen Mary by Name, according to the Apostles direction, to pray for all that are in Authority, which they visibly were; though I knew at the same time, this highly offended some, who refused the Oaths, and made me stand, in a manner, singly by my self.

I always opposed a Separation, and advised not a few, who thought fit to consult with me, to keep to the Communion of the Church; and not to entertain Prejudices against their Ministers for taking the Oath: for I was sensible of the Evil and Mischief of Schism, which some hot Men were then forward to promote, and are so still; witness a late Pamphlet in Answer to The Reasoning part of the Unreasonableness of the New Separation, which justifies a Schism now, upon such Principles, as would have made all the Jews Scismaticks, when the High Priesthood became Annual (though our Saviour himself then communicated with the Jewish Church) and makes the whole Greek Church Schismaticks, as often as the Grand Senior changes their Patriarch.

For I did not refuse the Oaths out of any fondness for the Government of King James, nor zeal for his Return; which, the present prospect of affairs gives no Man, who loves the Church of England, and the Liberties of his Country, any reason to wish: Nor yet out of any Aversion to the Government of King William and Queen Mary: but against my own Inclinations and Interest, out of pure Principles of Conscience,

to

The PREFACE.

to comply with the Obligations of my former Oaths, and that Duty which Subjects owe to their Prince, which I then apprehended irreconcileable with the new Oath.

This was a disposition of Mind prepared to receive satisfaction, when ever it was offered; and to comply chearfully with the present Government, when ever I could do it with a safe Conscience. I prayed heartily to God, that if I were in a mistake, he would let me see it; that I might not forfeit the Exercise of my Ministry, for a meer mistake: and I thank God, I have received that satisfaction which I desired; and if any Man can shew me, that the Principles I act on are false, uncertain, or precarious, and such as cannot reasonably satisfie an honest and unbiassed Mind, I will confess, that my desire of satisfaction has secretly and insensibly distorted my Judgment, though I took all possible care that it should not.

I find, the general Cry and Expectation is, that I should give my Reasons; though why I should be more obliged to give my Reasons for Swearing, than I was for not Swearing, I cannot tell.

Some seem very fond of this, upon a presumption that I can say nothing, but what they can easily Answer; and that will serve to expose Me, and the Cause together: I have for once gratified these Men, that they may have the opportunity to shew their skill.

Others, who are very well satisfied themselves, have yet a Curiosity to know what satisfied me, who have been so long dissatisfied. But this was no just Occasion to write Reasons; for if Reasons were never so plentiful with me, I can hardly think it worth the while to write a Book to gratifie a meer Curiosity.

There are others, who are still dissatisfied about the Oaths, and are desirous to try, Whether they can find that satisfaction, which I have done. This, I confess, is a good Reason, which may in Charity oblige me; and how hazardous an Attempt soever it be; my Duty to God, and to his Church, and to the Government, as well as Charity to my Brethren, seem to require it, when it is desired, and exacted from me: and I hope such Men will consider too, what is their Duty, as they will answer it to God, and to their own Consciences; to read what I have written for their sakes, carefully, and with an honest Mind; and to judge impartially; and whatever the Effect be, to take it kindly.

The PREFACE.

But there is another Motive has prevailed with me, more than all the rest: We live in an Age of great Prophaneness and Infidelity, which is ready to take all occasions to reproach Religion, and expose it, as a Cheat and Imposture, and to neglect no Opportunity to blacken the Clergy, as men of no Faith nor Religion themselves, though they make a great noise about it to serve their own Interests: And the general compliance of the Clergy in taking this New Oath, hath been improved by men of this Spirit to very ill purposes: And not only so, but some very Devout Christians have been greatly scandalized and offended at it: And others, who should have understood better, and checked this ill Temper, which is of such dangerous Consequence to Religion in general, have given too much countenance to it, and have seemed too much pleased, to see and hear all the Clergy that have taken this Oath, exposed to Contempt; as if, when the great Body of the Clergy is ridiculed and exposed, the Credit of Religion could be supported only by some few men, who refuse the Oath. Many of them indeed, to my knowledge, are very great and excellent Persons, whom I do from my heart Honour and Reverence, and whom I hope, and heartily pray, God will restore again to the Ministry of his Church: Yet I should be very sorry (and so I am sure, would they) that the Church and Religion should be reduced so low, as to be confined to their numbers; and have no firmer bottom to rest on than their Reputation, which though it be deservedly great, cannot bear the whole weight of the Church and Religion.

It is time to give check to such unchristian Censures, if we have any regard to our common Christianity: And since some little Writers among them (who are too head-strong to be governed by wiser men) engross the Church and Religion to themselves; and represent all who have taken the Oaths, especially the Clergy, as Apostates, at least from the Church of England, *if not from the Christian Faith; it is necessary to convince all sober Christians, that men may swear Allegiance to King* William *and Queen* Mary *without Perjury, and without renouncing any Principles of the Church of* England; *nay, that the Doctrine of the Church of* England *requires us to do so: And I hope, if this appear, their Zeal for the Church of* England, *if no other Consideration can prevail with them, will oblige them also to do it.*

But it seems, it will not serve my turn to offer such Reasons, as will justifie my compliance now, unless I can give a good Reason, why I did not take the Oaths before; that is, I must give such

Reasons

The PREFACE.

Reasons, as will equally prove, that no man ought to have taken the Oaths before, and that they ought to take them now.

These are very hard Task-Masters, and no doubt, have very kind Designs in it, to draw me in to provoke the Government by a needless justification of my self, as to what is past; which can serve no other end, but a little Vain-glory, that I would not be thought capable of a mistake; and lest the Non-swearers should not be Match enough for me, I must Proclaim War, and bid open Defiance to all that have taken this Oath; and prove, that they ought not to have sworn before I did, but were obliged to do it the very next minute.

But what now, if nothing of all this be necessary? What if I was not so well satisfied about this matter before, as I am now? Is any man forbidden to grow wiser, and upon a careful and thorough-examination of things, to alter his mind, when he sees good reason for it? I am not ashamed to own, that I am still a Learner; and hope, I shall be so, as long as I live, and improve my Knowledge every day by Study and Conversation.

So that without producing the Reasons of my dissatisfaction before, or being obliged to answer them, having never made them Publick, I think it very fair to give a satisfactory Reason now, for my taking of this Oath; hoping, that what hath satisfied me, may have the same effect upon some others, that will have the patience impartially to consider it.

I had indeed some of these Thoughts long since, which I drew up in Writing, and shewed to some of my Friends, and discoursed with others about them, and told them where I stuck: but stick I did, and could find no help for it; and there I had stuck to this day, had I not been relieved by *Bishop* Overal's Convocation-Book, which not only confirmed my former Notions, and suggested some new thoughts to me, which removed those Difficulties, which I could not before Conquer; but also by the Venerable Authority of a Covocation, gave me greater freedom and liberty of thinking, which the apprehensions of Novelty and Singularity had cramped before.

Thus, Reader, I have made Thee my Confessor, and declared my whole Heart to Thee, as to this Matter; and now judge of me, as Thou wouldst be judged by God another day.

I must add one thing more: That I have renounced no Principle that ever I taught, excepting one in The Case of Resistance, which P. 128,&c. is the only material Passage I know any reason to retract in that Book, viz. That when *St. Paul* says, All power is of God, he means only
Legal

The PREFACE.

Legal Powers; but that in an Hereditary Monarchy, where the right Heir is living, Usurped Powers are not of God, nor the Ordinance of God; as I proved by the Example of Joash: *The Reason and the Example you will find sufficiently answered in the following Discourse, and the Doctrine it self rejected by the Convocation; though it has been of late years so prevailing a mistake, and imposed by such great Authorities, that it is very pardonable, especially when it is so freely acknowledged: Though the truth is, I think still it is very true, as to the Case I then had in my Eye,* viz. *The Usurpations of the Rump Parliament,* &c. *but the fault is, that it is too generally expressed.*

In managing this Argument upon the Principles I have laid down, it is necessary to reason upon the Supposition of unjust Usurpations, and Illegal Revolutions of State; and it may be I may meet with some such Readers, as may charge me for so doing with Reflecting upon the present Government, which I am very sure, I am far from intending to do. And they who understand what belongs to Disputes of this Nature, know very well that the shortest way to bring the matter to an issue, is to put the Case at the worst that can be supposed; because this gives so much the greater force and advantage to the Argument, when it is suited to those, who are most strongly prejudiced against the Legality of the late Revolution: For supposing, but not granting, them to be in the right in this matter, I doubt not to make it appear, that it is for all that their Duty to swear Allegiance to the present Government, when required so to do: And this being clearly proved, it becomes altogether needless to debate the Legality of the late Revolution.

THE CONTENTS.

SECT. 1. *The Case plainly and briefly stated. That the Question, Whether Allegiance be due to a Prince, who is settled in the Throne, does not necessarily involve the Dispute about a Legal Right.* page 1

Sect. 2. *The Doctrine of the Church of England in this Point, as it is taught in Bishop* Overal's *Convocation Book.* 3

Two things proved from that Book: 1. *That those Princes, who have no Legal Right to their Thrones, may yet have Gods Authority.* 2. *That when they are throughly settled in their Thrones, they are invested with God's Authority, and must be reverenced and obeyed by all that live within their Territories and Dominions.* 5, &c.

Sect. 3. *The Testimony of Scripture and Reason in this Matter; reduced into several Propositions.* 10, &c.

Sect. 4. *Some Reasons and Arguments urged, and Objections Answered, for the further confirmation of this Doctrine.* 18

1. *That the Scripture has given us no direction in this Case, but to submit and pay all the Obedience of Subjects to the present Powers.* ibid.

Whether 13 Rom. 1, 2. *concern only Legal Powers.* 19

2. *This gives the easiest and most intelligible Account of the Original of Human Government; That all Power is from God.* 23

The several Hypotheses about the Original of Government considered, and shown ineffectual to found a Right, without resolving all into the Authority of God. ibid.

Object.

The CONTENTS.

Object. *This makes a King lose his Right, by being notoriously injured*, 25. *Answer* 26

Concerning the Oaths of Allegiance. 27,&c,

Object. *This Doctrine makes it impossible for an injured Prince to recover his Right. Answered.* 32

Object. *This encourages Ambitious Spirits to grasp at Crowns. Answered.* 33

Object. *That Pyrates and Robbers have as good a Title to our Purse as Usurpers to the Crown. Answered.* 34

Object. *The Case of* Jehoiada's *anointing* Joash, *and killing* Athaliah. *Answered.* ibid.

Object. *That all Kings are not set up by God, proved from* Hosea 8. 4. *Answered.* 35

3. *This Doctrine is founded on the same Principle with the Doctrine of Non-Resistance and Passive Obedience.* 36

4. *To deny this is to deny God's Authority to remove Kings, and to set up Kings.* 37

5. *It limits God's Providence in governing Kings, and protecting innocent and injured Subjects.* ibid.

6. *The necessity of Government to preserve Human Societies, proves this.* 38

Bishop Sanderson's *Opinion about Submission to Usurped Powers, examined.* ibid.

7. *These Principles answer all the ends of Government, both for the Security of the Prince and Subjects.* 43

An Answer to a great Prejudice, that these Principles will equally serve all Usurpations, with a particular respect to the Rebellion in 1640. 45

The Objection from the Laws of the Land considered, and some brief Remarks on a late Book, entituled, The Case of Allegiance to a King in Possession. *p.* 51. 55.

THE CASE OF THE ALLEGIANCE DUE TO Sovereign Powers, &c.

SECT. I.

The Case plainly and briefly stated.

THAT which has perplexed this Controversie, is the intermixing the Dispute of *Right* with the Duty of *Obedience*, or making the *Legal Right* of Princes to their Thrones the only Reason and Foundation of *the Allegiance* of Subjects: That Allegiance is due only to *Right*, not to *Government*, though it can be paid only to Government. Many of those who have writ in defence of the New Oath, have supposed this, that a Legal Right is necessary to make Allegiance due, and therefore have endeavoured to justifie the Legal Right of Their present Majesties: This as I have shewn it to be unnecessary; so it seems to me to be unfit to dispute the Right of Princes; a thing which no Government can permit to be a Question among their Subjects: And how well soever such Disputes

B may

The Case of the Allegiance

may be intended, they are certainly needless in this Cause, and serve only to confound it, by carrying men into such dark Labyrinths of Law and History, &c. as very few know how to find their way out of again: And therefore I shall not meddle with this Dispute, as being both above me, and nothing to my present purpose.

And on the other hand, those also, who refuse the New Oath, go wholly upon this Principle, That Allegiance is due only to a Legal Right. And take away that, and you remove all the difficulties they labour under. They think, that a rightful Prince only has Right to our Allegiance. That though he be dispossessed of his Throne, if ever he had Right to it, he has Right still; and therefore our Duty is still owing to him, and to no other; and our Oaths of Allegiance to him still bind us: and that no other Prince, who ascends the Throne without a Legal Right, has Right to our Allegiance; and that to swear Allegiance to him, while we are under the Obligation of a former Oath to our rightful Prince, is Perjury.

As far as I know, this is the sum of all that can be said in this Cause: Allowing these Principles, there is no way to satisfie such men, but by justifying the Legality of the late Revolution. But though many things are said, which may make men much more modest in the point than some are; yet to judge truly of this requires such perfect Skill in Law and History, and the Constitution of the *English* Government, that few men are capable of making so plain and certain a judgment of it, as to be a clear and safe Rule of Conscience.

But if the Principle be false, there is an end of the Dispute: And Subjects have a plain Rule of Duty without understanding Laws and Politicks, the Intrigues of Government, the Revolutions of States, the Disputes of Princes; which I am sure is both for the security of Governments and Subjects.

If then Allegiance be due, not for the sake of Legal Right, but Government.

If Allegiance be due, not to bare Legal Right, but to the Authority of God.

If God, when he sees fit, and can better serve the ends of his Providence by it, sets up Kings without any regard to Legal Right, or Humane Laws.

If

due to Soveraign Powers, &c.

If Kings, thus set up by God, are invested with Gods Authority, which must be obeyed, not only for wrath, but also for conscience sake.

If these Principles be true, it is plain, that Subjects are bound to obey, and to pay and swear Allegiance (if it be required) to those Princes whom God hath placed and settled in the Throne, whatever Disputes there may be about their legal Right, when they are invested with God's Authority.

And then it is plain, that our old Allegiance and old Oaths are at an end, when God has set over us a new King: for when God transfers Kingdoms, and requires our Obedience and Allegiance to a new King, he necessarily transfers our Allegiance too.

This Scheme of Government may startle some men at first, before they have well considered it. But every One at first sight must acknowledge, that it is so much for the ease and safety of Subjects in all Revolutions (which very frequently happen) what the generality of Mankind, from an inward principle of Self-preservation, have always done, and will always do, that they have reason to wish it to be true, and to be glad to see it well proved.

And this I shall endeavour to do from the Authority of Scripture and Reason; and that I may not appear to be singular in it, and to advance Paradoxes, I shall prove it likewise from the Doctrine and Principles of the Church of *England*.

SECT. II.

The Doctrine of the Church of England *in this Point, as it is taught in Bishop* Overal's *Convocation Book.*

I Shall begin with the Doctrine of the Church of *England*, not that I equal, much less prefer it, before the Scripture; but because some, who refuse the Oath, lay great stress on it, and upon this score charge their Brethren with no less then Apostasie from the Church; and possibly when such a venerable Authority stands in the Front, it will prepare a kinder Reception for the Reasons, which follow.

The Case of the Allegiance

The Church of *England* has been very careful to instruct Her Children in their Duty to Princes; to obey their Laws, and submit to their Power, and not to resist, though very injuriously oppressed; and those, who renounce these Principles, renounce the Doctrine of the Church of *England*: But she has withal taught, That all Soveraign Princes receive their Power and Authority from God; and therefore every Prince, who is setled in the Throne, is to be obeyed and reverenced as God's Minister, and not to be resisted; which directs us what to do in all Revolutions of Government, when once they come to a Settlement; and those who refuse to pay and swear Allegiance to such Princes, whom God has placed in the Throne, whatever their legal right be, do as much reject the Doctrine of the Church of *England*, as those who teach the Resistance of Princes.

For the proof of which, I appeal to Bishop *Overal's* Convocation Book, which contains the Acts and Canons of the Convocation begun in the first Year of King *James* I. 1603. and continued by Adjournments and Prorogations to 1610. under Archbishop *Bancroft*, a wise and learned man.

Page 57.   In *Chapt*. 28. the Convocation having given an Account of the various and irregular Revolutions of Government, brought about by the Providence of God, " who for the sins of any Nati-
" on or Country, altereth their Governments and Governours,
" transferreth, setteth up, and bestoweth Kingdoms, as it seemeth
" best to his heavenly wisdom, they add these remarkable words; *And when having attained their ungodly desires (whether ambitious Kings, by bringing any Country into their Subjection; or disloyal Subjects, by their rebellious rising against their Natural Soveraigns) they have established any of the same degenerate Forms of Government among their People; the Authority either so unjustly gotten, or wrung by force from the true and lawful Possessor, being always God's Authority (and therefore receiving no Impeachment by the wickedness of those that have it) is ever (when any such Alterations are throughly settled) to be reverenced and obeyed, and the People of all sorts, (as well of the Clergy, as of the Laity) are to be subject unto it, not only for wrath, but also for conscience sake.*

Page 59.   In *Can*. 28. where this Doctrine is decreed, they take care to condemn all those wicked means whereby such Changes of Governments are made, and yet to assert, That whenever such Changes are made, the Authority is Gods, and must be obeyed.
" If any man therefore shall affirm, either that the Subjects, when
" they

due to Soveraign Powers, &c.

"they shake off the Yoke of their Obedience to their Soveraigns, and set up a Form of Government among themselves, after their own Humours, do not therein very wickedly: or that it is lawful for any bordering Kings, through Ambition and Malice, to invade their Neighbours: or that the Providence and Goodness of God, in using of Rebellions and Oppressions against any King or Country, doth mitigate or qualifie the Offences of any such Rebels or oppressing Kings: or that when any such new Forms of Government, begun by Rebellion, and after throughly settled, the Authority in them is not of God: or that any, who live within the Territories of such new Governments, are not bound to be subject to God's Authority, which is there executed, but may rebel against the same: or that the *Jews* in *Egypt* or *Babylon* might lawfully, for any Cause, have taken Arms against any of those Kings, or have offered any violence to their Persons, he doth greatly err."

Men may dispute any thing, but I know not how it was possible for the Convocation to express their sense plainer, that all usurped Powers, when throughly settled, have God's Authority, and must be obeyed: So that here are the Two great Points determined, whereon this whole Controversie turns.

1. That those Princes, who have no legal right to their Thrones, may yet have God's Authority.

2. That when they are throughly settled in their Thrones, they are invested with God's Authority, and must be reverenced and obeyed by all, who live within their Territories and Dominions, as well Priests, as People: If these Propositions be true, it is a plain Resolution of the Case; that if it should at any time happen, that the rightful Prince should be driven out of his Kingdom, and another Prince placed in his Throne, and settled in the full Administration of Government, Subjects not only may, but must for conscience sake, and out of reverence to the Authority of God, with which such a Prince is invested, pay all the Duty and Allegiance of Subjects to him.

As for the first, the Case is plain, that the Convocation speaks of illegal and usurped Powers, and yet affirms that the Authority exercised by them, is God's Authority, and therefore those Princes, who have no legal right, may have God's Authority: the words of the Canon are very plain and express, and yet if any man desires further satisfaction, that this was the Judgment of the

The Case of the Allegiance

the Convocation, that Princes, who have no Legal Right, may have God's Authority, it is very easie to give it.

Page 46. They teach, That *the Lord* (in advancing Kings to their Thrones) *is not bound to those Laws, which he prescribeth others to observe,* and therefore *commanded* Jehu *a Subject to be anointed King over* Israel, *of purpose to punish the sins of* Ahab *and* Jezebel: and what he did by Prophets in *Israel*, by an express Nomination of the Person, he does by his Providence in other Kingdoms, set up Kings when he sees fit, without any regard to the Right of

Page 53. Succession, or Legal Titles. For as they tell us elsewhere, *The Lord both may, and is able to overthrow any Kings or Emperors, notwithstanding any Claim, Right, Title, or Interest, which they can challenge to their Countries, Kingdoms, or Empires.*

The *Moabites* and *Aramites* never could have a Legal Right to the Government of *Israel*, and yet the Convocation asserts, That

Page 51. when *Israel* was in subjection to them, *they knew, that it was not lawful for them of themselves, and by their own Authority to take Arms against the Kings, whose Subjects they were, though indeed they were Tyrants.* And that it *had not been lawful for* Ehud *to have killed King* Eglon, *had he not been first made by God the Judge, Prince, and Ruler of the People.*

The like, we see, they teach of the Kings of *Egypt* and *Babylon*, who never had a Legal and Natural Right to Govern *Israel*; and the like they affirm of the *Four Monarchies*, which were all violent Usurpations; and the Principle they ground this on, plainly extends to all Kings and Soveraign Princes: That God, and his

Ch. 35. Son Jesus Christ, *who is the Universal Lord and Ruler over all the*
page 83. *World,* does remove and set up Kings, as will best serve the Ends
Jer. 27. 5. of his wise Providence. *I have made (saith he) the Earth, the Man, and the Beasts that are upon the ground, and have given it to whom it pleaseth me.* And again, the Prophet Daniel *telleth us, That God changeth the Times and the Seasons, that he hath Power, and beareth*
4 Dan. 17. *Rule over the Kingdoms of Men: that he taketh away Kings, and set-*
32. *teth up Kings; and that it was the God of Heaven, who gave unto*
2 Dan. 37. Nebuchadnezzar *so great a Kingdom, Power, Strength, and Glory, as then he had, to Rule with Majesty and Honour a very great Empire: in respect whereof, although Kings and Princes might have been satisfied with the Titles of Lieutenants, or Vicegerents on Earth, to the Son of God; yet he did communicate and impart so much of his Power, Authority, and Dignity unto them, as he was content to stile them with his own Name; I have said ye are Gods, and the Children of the most*

most High. And therefore we may obferve, there is no Duty Subjects, as fuch, owe to the moft Legal and Rightful Kings, but the *Convocation* afferts due to all Kings, whom God hath placed in the Throne, by what vifible means foever they obtained it: as to obey and fubmit to them, not to refift them, nor rebel againft them, to pay all Cuftoms and Taxes, to pray for them, nay, to fwear Allegiance to them, if it be required.

Thus they teach with refpect to *Alexander* (and I think any Prince who gets the Throne, may pretend as much Right to it, as he). *If any Man therefore fhall affirm, either that the Jews,* gene-*Can.* 31. *rally, both Priefts and People, were not the Subjects of* Alexander, *af-* page 67. *ter his Authority was fetled amongft them, as they had been before the Subjects of the Kings of* Babylon *and* Perfia; *or that they might lawfully have born Arms againft him; or that they were not all bound to pray for the long Life and Profperity, both of* Alexander, *and his Empire, as they had been before to pray for the Life and Profperity of the other faid Kings, and their Kingdoms, while they lived under their Subjection: or confequently, that they might lawfully, upon any occafion whatfoever, have offered Violence and Deftruction, either to their Perfons, or to their Kingdoms,* &c. *he doth greatly err.*

Thus *Can.* 33. they teach, That whoever affirms, *That the* Page 78. *Jews were not bound, both to have paid their Tribute, and to have prayed for* Cæfar *without diffimulation, fincerely and truly, notwithftanding any pretence of Tyranny, which they had wilfully drawn upon their own heads, or of any caufe whatfoever; or that fuch as curfed* Cæfar, *(their chief Governour) did not thereby deferve any corporal punifhment, which is due to be inflicted upon fuch Traitors; or that the Rebellion againft Any King, Abfolute Prince, or Civil Magiftrate, for any caufe whatfoever, is not a fin deteftable in the fight of God,* &c. *he doth greatly err.*

Chapter 34. they condemn the *Pharifees,* who when Herod upon Page 79. occafion caufed his Subjects to bind themfelves by Oath, *Quòd non deceffuri effent à fide & officio,* refufed to take that Oath. And in their 34th *Canon* they teach: That *if any Man affirm, That the Phari-* Page 82. *fees in refufing to bind their Allegiance and Faith to* Cæfar, *by an Oath, did not thereby fhew themfelves traitreroufly affected towards him (which evidently is not true of all, who may refufe fuch Oath, but the intention is only to condemn fuch a refufal); or that it was not a feditious Doctrine——To refufe all Taxations impofed by the* Romans, *their lawful Magiftrates, and rather to rebel than to pay any Tribute to them,* &c. *he doth greatly err.*

The Case of the Allegiance

In the Case of *Jaddus* swearing Allegiance to *Darius*, they condemn those, who say, That Jaddus *the High-Priest did amiss in binding his Allegiance to King* Darius *by Oath, or that he had not sinned, if he had refused (being thereunto required) to have sworn.* And yet in the very next *Canon*, which I have already quoted, they teach, That both *Priests* and *People* (and therefore *Jaddus* himself) became as much the Subjects of *Alexander*, as they had been of *Darius*; and then according to this Doctrine, if *Alexander* had required an Oath of *Allegiance* from *Jaddus*, (as it is probable he did) *Jaddus* had sinned, if he had refused that Oath, though according to all the Circumstances of the Story, *Darius* was then living, to whom *Jaddus* had before sworn Allegiance.

Can. 30. *page* 65.

Page 64.

But it will be objected against this, that the *Convocation* takes notice of that Answer *Jaddus* gave to *Alexander*, when he sent to him from *Tyre*, after the Overthrow of *Darius*, That *he should assist him in his Wars, and become Tributary to the* Macedonians, *as he had been to the* Persians: *He returned for his Answer, That he might not yield to this, because he had taken an Oath for his true Allegiance to* Darius, *which he might not lawfully violate, while* Darius *lived, being by flight escaped, when his Army was discomfited.* But we may observe, that the *Convocation* in their *Canon* upon it, takes no notice, that *Jaddus* having sworn to *Darius*, could not submit, or swear to any other Prince, while *Darius* lived; and it is plain, *Jaddus* himself did not mean this by it, for he immediately submitted to *Alexander*, as soon as he came to *Jerusalem*, before he had given the last fatal Overthrow to *Darius*, when *Darius* in his flight was murdered by his own Servants. The meaning then of *Jaddus*'s Answer to *Alexander*, was no more but this: That he having sworn Allegiance to *Darius*, could not make a voluntary dedition of himself to *Alexander*, which was the thing desired; but when he was in *Alexander*'s Power, (which made it a matter of force, not of his own choice) he made no scruple to submit to *Alexander*, and become his Subject and Tributary, as he formerly was the sworn Subject of *Darius*.

Page 65.

This, I think, sufficiently proves the first thing, that this *Convocation* taught, That Princes, who have no Legal Right to their Thrones, when they are placed there by God, are invested with God's Authority, and must be reverenced and obeyed by all Subjects, in as full a manner, as any other the most legal and rightful Prince can challenge.

2*dly*,

due to Sovereign Powers, &c.

2*dly*, The only Enquiry then is, what the Convocation means by the Government's being *throughly setled*. A Prince, who is throughly setled in his Throne, has God's Authority, and must be obeyed; but when is his Government throughly setled?

Now here it is, that men may impose upon themselves, if they will, and if they think it their Interest to do so; and may make as little or as much go to a through settlement, as they please; for the *Convocation* has not determined the bounds of it: they thought this a visible thing, that every Subject could see, when the Government is so setled, as to make our Obedience due and necessary, and therefore there was no need of defining, what it is to be throughly setled: When the whole administration of Government, and the whole power of the Nation is in the hands of the Prince; when every thing is done in his Name, and by his Authority; when the Estates of the Realm, and the great Body of the Nation has submitted to him, and those who will not submit, can be crushed by him, when ever he pleases; if this be not a setled Government, I despair of ever knowing what it is; for there is no Government in the World so setled, but that by some unseen Accident, or by greater Force and Power, it may be unsetled; and in this sense it is impossible ever to know, when a Government is setled; for no Goverment is, or can be thus setled against all events: but then the Government is visibly setled, when the Prince has the full and perfect Administration of all Affairs relating to his Kingdom.

But if the general submission of the People settle a Government, I am sure, that is easily enough known, when a Nation has submitted to a Prince; but this will not be allowed us, that the submission of the People settles the Government, unless the Prince, who has the Right to Govern, submit also; but I would gladly hear a good Reason for this: The submission of the Prince indeed may be thought necessary to transfer a Legal Right; but the submission of the People, of it self, is sufficient to settle a Government, and when it is setled, then it is the Authority of God, whatever the Humane Right be.

This I take to be the true sense of this *Convocation* concerning Obedience to Sovereign Powers; all Sovereign Powers, whose Power and Goverment is *throughly setled*, must be obeyed, whatever their Legal Right be; for they have the Authority of God, to which our Obedience and Subjection is due, and that supersedes all further enquiries. This is a good Argument

from

from Authority, and as good Authority as can be urged to the Members of the Church of *England*; for if a *Convocation* cannot declare the Judgment of the Church of *England*, I know not whence we shall learn it.

But I will not rely only upon Authority, but I think so great an Authority, if it do not determine our judgment, ought at least to make us more carefully and impartially to examine the Reasons of things, and to deliver us from the Tyranny of Præpossession and Prejudice; and to that I proceed.

SECT. III.

The Testimony of Scripture *and* Reason *in this matter.*

THat which we are to' prove, is, That all Sovereign Princes, who are setled in their Thrones, are placed there by God, and invested with his Authority, and therefore must be obeyed by all Subjects, as the Ministers of God, without enquiring into their Legal Right and Title to the Throne: The Proofs of this from Scripture and Reason must necessarily be intermixt and interwoven with each other; and to set this matter in as clear a Light as I can, I shall reduce the whole into some plain Propositions.

Prop. 1. That all Civil Power and Authority is from God; for he is the Supreme Lord of the World, and has the sole Right to Govern his Creatures, and therefore no man can have any Authority but from God: this will be readily acknowledged by all, who believe, that there is a God, and that he made and governs the World.

Prop. 2. That Civil Power and Authority is no otherwise from God, then as he gives this Power and Authority to some particular Person or Persons, to Govern others: For Authority belongs to a Person, and that Power and Authority, which any Person exercises, is not from God, which God never gave him: If he Governs without receiving his Personal Authority from God, he Governs without God's Authority.

I take

due to Sovereign Powers, &c.

I take notice of this to prevent a common Evasion, that all Power is said to *be of God*, because God has instituted Civil Authority; not that every one, who exercises this Authority, receives it from God.

But what they mean by the Institution of Civil Authority, I cannot tell, unless it be, that God intended, that Mankind should live under Government: but this does not prove, that all Power and Authority is from God, unless those, who exercise this Authority, receive it from God: And it is plain, that St. *Paul*, 13 *Rom.* 1. by the *Higher Powers*, and *all power*, means those, who exercise this Supreme Power, that all such Soveraign Princes are set up by God, and receive their Authority from him; they are the *Rulers*, v. 3. *the Ministers of God, who bear the Sword*, v. 4. and in St. *Peter*, *the King as Supreme*, 1 *Pet.* 2. 13.

Prop. 3. There are but three ways whereby God gives this Power and Authority to any Persons: Either by Nature, or by an express Nomination, or by the disposals of Providence.

By Nature: Parents have a Natural Superiority over their Children, and are their Lords and Governours too: This was the first Government in the World, and is the only Natural Authority; for in propriety of speaking, there is no Natural Prince but a Father. But by what bounds this paternal and Patriarchal Authority was limited, we cannot tell; how the extent of their power was stinted, and where new Families, and new Governments began; and it is in vain for us to enquire after it now.

By a particular Nomination: God made Kings only in *Jewry*, and entailed the Kingdom of *Judah* upon *David's* Posterity: and after the Division of the *Ten Tribes* from the Kingdom of *Judah*, by express Nomination set *Jeroboam* and *Jehu* over the Kingdom of *Israel*.

But God ruled in all the other Kingdoms of the World, as well as in *Jewry*, and all other Kings ruled by God's Authority, as well as the Kings of *Judah* and *Israel*, who were advanced by his Command: *For the most high ruleth in the Kingdom of men, and giveth it to whomsoever he will, and setteth up over it the basest of men,* 4 Dan. 17. *It was the God of Heaven, that gave* Nebuchadnezzar *a Kingdom, Power, and Strength, and Glory. It is he, that changeth times and seasons, that removeth Kings, and setteth up Kings,* 2 Dan. 21. 37. and the Prophecy of the *four Monarchies* is a demonstration of it.

C 2 But

The Case of the Allegiance

But now God governs the rest of the world, removeth Kings, and setteth up Kings, only by his Providence; that is, then God sets up a King, when by his Providence he advances him to the Throne, and puts the Soveraign Authority into his hands; then he removeth a King, when by his Providence he thrusts him from his Throne, and takes the Government out of his hands: for Providence is God's Government of the world by an invisible influence and power, whereby he directs, determines, over-rules all Events to the accomplishment of his own Will and Counsels, in distinction from his more visible Government by his *Oracles* and *Prophets*, or the express significations of his Will, as he in former Ages governed *Israel*.

Nor does it make any difference in this Case to distinguish between what God permits, and what he does; for this distinction does not relate to the Events of things, but to the wickedness of men; which is the only reason for this distinction; for the Scripture never speaks of God's bare permission of any Events, but makes him the Author of all the good or evil which happens either to private persons, or publick Societies. The Events of all things are in his hands, and are ordered and disposed by his Will and Counsel, as they must be if God governs the world: but God cannot be the Author of any wickedness, cannot inspire men with any wicked counsels or designs, nor incline their wills to the commission of it, and therefore this we say God only permits; but when it comes to action, he over-rules their wicked designs to accomplish his own Counsels and Decrees; and either disappoints what they intended, or gives success to them, when he can serve the ends of his Providence by their wickedness: and herein consists the unsearchable wisdom of Providence, that God brings about his own Counsels by the free Ministries of men: He permits men to do wickedly, but all Events, which are for the good or evil of private men, or publick Societies, are ordered by him, as the Prophet declares, *Amos* 3.6. *Shall there be evil in a City, and the Lord hath not done it.*

And yet if there were any such distinction as this, that some Events God only permits, and some he orders and appoints, we ought in reason to ascribe the advancement of Kings to God's decree and counsel, because it is the principal act of Providence, which has so great an influence upon the government of the world; and if he decree and order any Events, certainly he peculiarly orders such Events as will do most good or most hurt to
the

due to Soveraign Powers, &c. 13

the world. He muſt with his own hand immediately direct the motions of the great wheels of Providence; and not permit them to move as they pleaſe themſelves. Eſpecially when we remember, that Kings are God's Miniſters and Lieutenants, and are inveſted with his Authority: Now to give Authority to any perſon, does not ſignifie to permit him to take it; and we cannot but think that God will exerciſe a particular care and providence in appointing his great Miniſters. No man can have God's Authority, but he to whom it is given; and if the advancement to the Throne inveſts ſuch a Prince with God's Authority, then God gives him the Throne, and does not meerly permit him to take it; for no man can take God's Authority, but it muſt be given.

Nay, ſince God makes Kings now, not by an expreſs nomination of any perſons, but only by the Events of Providence, we muſt not allow, that God at any time permits men to make themſelves Kings, whom he does not make Kings: for then we can never diſtinguiſh between Kings by the permiſſion and by the appointment of God, between God's Kings, and Kings of their own making; unleſs all Kings are ſet up by God, and inveſted with his Authority, we can never know what King's have God's Authority, who thoſe are, whom we muſt obey out of Conſcience, and whom we muſt not obey: there is no direction how to diſtinguiſh them, and the Events of Providence in placing them in the Throne, are the ſame in both.

Now the neceſſary Conſequence of this is, that by what means ſoever any Prince aſcends the Throne, he is placed there by God, and receives his Authority from him. There are very different ways indeed, whereby this is done; ſometimes by the Election of the people; ſometimes by Conqueſt (which has been the viſible Original of moſt Governments) and when any Family is thus advanced to the Throne, it is continued by Succeſſion and legal Entails; but all theſe ways, or any other, that can be thought of, are governed and determined by the Divine Providence, and the Prince thus advanced is as truly placed in the Throne by God, as if he had been expreſly nominated, and anointed by a *Prophet* at God's command, as *Saul* and *David* were. Sometimes God leaves a free People to chooſe their own King, and then he directs their choice to ſuch a perſon as he will make King. Sometimes he ſuffers an aſpiring Prince to invade and conquer a Country, but he never ſuffers him to aſcend the Throne, but when he ſees fit to make him

King.

The Case of the Allegiance

King. Sometimes he not only places a single Person in the Throne, but entails it on his Family by Human Laws, and makes the Throne a legal Inheritance; but when he sees cause for it, he interrupts the Succession, or finally transfers the Kingdom to another Family.

Prop. 4. All Kings are equally rightful with respect to God: for those are all rightful Kings, who are placed in the Throne by God, and it is impossible there should be a wrong King, unless a man could make himself King, whether God will or no. The whole Authority of Government is Gods, and whoever has God's Authority is a true and rightful King; for he has the true and rightful Authority of a King; and if all Kings, who are settled and established in their Thrones, are set up by God, and have his Authority, with respect to the Authority which they have from God, they are rightful Kings.

Prop. 5. The distinction then between a King *de jure*, and a King *de facto*, relates only to Human Laws, which bind Subjects, but are not the necessary Rules and Measures of the Divine Providence. In Hereditary Kingdoms, He is a rightful King, who has by Succession a legal Right to the Crown; and He who has possession of the Crown, without a legal Right, is a King *de facto*; that is, is a King, but not by Law: Now Subjects are so tied up by the Constitutions of the Kingdom, that they must not pull down or set up Kings contrary to the Laws of the Land; but God is not bound by Human Laws, but can make whom he pleases King, without regard to legal Rights, and when he does so, they are true, though not legal Kings, if those are true Kings who have God's Authority.

Prop. 6. We can have but one King at a time: two rival and opposite Princes cannot at the same time possess the same Throne, nor can Subjects be bound to two opposite and contrary Allegiances; for *no man can serve two Masters*; and yet Allegiance is due to a King by the Laws of God, and to every King whose Subjects we are, that if we could have two Kings, we must have two Allegiances.

Prop. 7. He is our King who is settled in the Throne in the actual Administration of Soveraign Power: for *King* is the Name of Power and Authority, not of meer Right. He, who has a legal Right to the Crown, but has it not, ought by the Laws of the Land to be King, but is not: but he, who is actually settled in the Administration of the Regal Power, is King, and has God's Authority, though he have not a legal Right.

But

But the Objection against this is, That it is *Hobbism*, that Dominion is naturally annexed to Power; but those who say this, do not understand Mr. *Hobbs*, or me: for He makes Power, and nothing else, to give Right to Dominion; and therefore asserts, That God himself is the Natural Lord and Governour of the World, not because he made it; but because he is Omnipotent; but I say, That Government is founded in Right, and that God is the Natural Lord of the World, because he made it; and that no Creature has any Right to Govern the World, or any part of it, but as he receives Authority from God: and therefore since Power will Govern, God so orders it by his Providence, as never to intrust Soveraign Power in any Mans hands, to whom he does not give the Soveraign Authority: that Power does not give Right and Authority to Govern, but is a certain sign to us, that where God has placed and settled the Power, he has given the Authority.

Prop. 8. Allegiance is due only to the King: for Allegiance signifies all that Duty, which Subjects owe to their King, and therefore can be due to none but the King.

If then he who has the Legal Right may not be our King, and he who has not, may; when any such Case happens, we must pay our Allegiance to him who is King, though without a Legal Right; not to him who is not our King, though it is his Right to be so: And the reason is very plain, because Allegiance is due only to God's Authority, not to a bare Legal Title without God's Authority; and therefore must be paid to him who is invested with God's Authority, who is his Minister and Lieutenant; that is, to the Actual King, who is setled in the Throne, and has the Administration of Government in his hands.

Object. But if this be so, what does a Legal Right signifie, if it do not command the Allegiance of Subjects?

Answ. I answer: It barrs all other Humane Claims: No other Prince can challenge the Throne of Right: and Subjects are bound to maintain the Rights of such a Prince, as far as they can; that is, against all Mankind; but not against God's disposal of Crowns: and therefore when God transfers the Kingdom, he transfers our Allegiance, which is due, and annexed to his Authority, whether this Authority be conveyed by a Legal Succession, or by any other means.

Object.

The Case of the Allegiance

Object. But if we have sworn Allegiance to such a Prince, and his Heirs, and lawful Successors, how can we pay Allegiance to any other Prince, while He, or any of his Heirs, and Legal Successors are living, and claim our Allegiance, without violating our Oaths?

Answ. I answer: An Oath of Allegiance made to any King, can oblige no longer than he continues to be King; for if it did, it would oblige us against our Duty, and so become an unlawful Oath: for our Allegiance is due to him who is King, in the actual and setled possession of the Throne, and therefore must by the Law of God be paid there; and then it cannot be paid to the dispossessed Prince, unless we can have two Allegiances: Our Oath then to the dispossessed Prince ceases, *Cessante materiâ*; for though the Man is in being still, the King is gone.

But we swear to maintain and defend his Right, and the Right of his Heirs: but yet we do not swear to keep them in the Throne, which may be impossible for us to do against a prosperous Rebellion; nor do we swear in Case they are thrown out of the Throne, never to submit or pay Allegiance to any other Prince; which would be an unlawful Oath, as contrary to that Duty we owe to the Divine Providence in making Kings, and removing Kings. The Oath of Allegiance contains the Duty of Subjects to their King, and can extend no farther, and therefore can oblige no longer than he is our King, and we his Subjects.

These seem to me, to be very plain *Propositions*, and to carry their own Evidence with them; and if this be true, it is a very plain Direction to Subjects in all the Revolutions of Government.

The most that can be expected from them, according to the strictest Principles of Loyalty and Obedience, is to have no hand in such Revolutions, or to oppose them as far as they can, and not to be hasty and forward in their Compliances; but when such a Revolution is made, and they cannot help it; they must reverence and obey their New Prince, as invested with God's Authority.

Nor is it very hard to know, when our Obedience becomes due to a New Prince; for it does not consist in a Mathematical point, nor require Mathematical certainty: Our Obedience is due to God's Authority, and when we can reasonably conclude, that God has made him King; that is, when the Providence of God has setled him in the Throne, we must pay our Obedience to him.

There

due to Soveraign Powers, &c.

There are different degrees of Settlement, and must necessarily be in such new Governments, which seem to me to require different degrees of Submission, or at least to justifie them, till it increases to such a full and plenary and settled possession, as requires our Allegiance, as being notoriously evident and sensible to all that do not wink hard, and will not see it.

If the generality of the Nation submit to such a Prince, and place him on the Throne, and put the whole power of the Kingdom into his hands, though it may be, we cannot yet think the Providence of God has settled him in the Throne, while the dispossessed Prince has also such a formidable power, as makes the Event very doubtful, yet if we think fit to continue in the Kingdom, under the government and power of the new Prince, there are several Duties, which in reason we ought to pay him.

As to live quietly and peaceably under his government, and to promise, or swear, or give any other security that we will do so, if it be demanded: It is reasonable we should do so, if we think it reasonable to live under the protection of the government; this all men do in an Enemies quarters, and no man blames them for it.

We must pay Taxes to them; for these are due to the Administration of government, as St. *Paul* observes; *For this cause pay ye Tribute also, for they are the Ministers of God, attending continually on this very thing,* 13 Rom. 6. And if we owe our secure possession of our Estates to the protection of government, let the government be what it will, we ought to pay for it.

We must give the Title of King to such a Prince, when we live in the Country where he is owned for King; for besides that it is a piece of good manners (which is the least thing we can owe to him, under whose government we live) he is indeed King, while he administers the Regal power, though we may not think him so well settled in his government, as to all intents and purposes to own him for our King.

Nay, we must pray for him under the Name and Title of King, for we are bound to pray for all who are in Authority; and that a Prince is, who has the whole government in his hands, and has power to do a great deal of hurt, or a great deal of good; and this is so far from being a fault, that it is a duty, while we take care to do it in such terms, as not to pray against the dispossessed Prince.

D Thus

Thus far I think the doubtful poſſeſſion of the Throne obliges us, and it were very happy if no more were required in the beginnings of ſuch a new government; but when beſides the poſſeſſion of the Throne, the power of the diſpoſſeſſed Prince is broken, and no viſible proſpect of his recovering his Throne again; nay, if it be viſible that he can never recover his Throne again, but by making a new Conqueſt of the Nation by Foreigners, who will be our Maſters, if they conquer, and no very gentle ones neither; we may then look upon the new Prince as advanced and ſettled by God in his Throne, and therefore ſuch a King, as we owe an entire Obedience and Allegiance to.

For we muſt not take the conſideration of Right into the ſettlement of Government; for a Prince may be ſettled in his Throne without legal Right, and when he is ſo, God has made him our King, and requires our Obedience.

Theſe principles are ſo very uſeful, eſpecially in all Revolutions of government, that Subjects have great reaſon to wiſh them true, and to examine over again thoſe ſtrict principles of Loyalty, which if purſued to their juſt conſequences, muſt unavoidably in ſome Junctures, ſacrifice whole Kingdoms, at leaſt all Subjects who pretend to this degree and kind of Loyalty and Conſcience, to the ill Fortune of their Prince.

SECT. IV.

Some Reaſons and Arguments urged, and Objections anſwered, for the further Confirmation of this Doctrine.

THat we may examine this more impartially and more ſecurely rely upon the Dictates of Reaſon in this matter, I obſerve,

1. That the Scripture has given us no Directions in this Caſe, but to ſubmit, and pay all the Obedience of Subjects to the preſent powers. It makes no diſtinction, that ever I could find, between rightful Kings and Uſurpers, between Kings whom we muſt, and whom we muſt not obey; but the general Rule is, *Let every Soul be ſubject to the higher Powers, for all power is of God, the Powers that be are ordained of God: whoſoever therefore reſiſteth the Power, reſiſteth the Ordinance of God, and they that reſiſt ſhall receive to them-*

due to Soveraign Powers, &c.

themselves damnation, 13 Rom. 1, 2. To say the *Apostle* here speaks of lawful powers, is *gratìs dictum*, for there is no Evidence of it: The Criticism between ἐξυσία and δύναμις will not do; for they both signifie the same thing in Scripture, either force and power, or authority: ἐκ ἐγὼ ἐξυσιασθήσομαι ὑπό τινός. *I will not be brought under the power of any thing,* must signifie force, 1 Cor. 6. 12. and δύναμις must signifie authority and dignity, 1 Eph. 21. ὑπεράνω πάσης ἀρχῆς ᾗ ἐξυσίας ᾗ δυνάμεως ᾗ κυριότητ[Θ]-, which are several names and degrees of dignity and authority, as well as power. Κυριεύων and ἐξυσιάζειν signifie the same thing, the exercise of civil authority and power, 22 *Luke* 25. and therefore οἱ ἐξυσίαι are the οἱ ἐξυσιάζοντες, those who exercise authority and dominion; the οἱ ἄρχοντες, *the Rulers,* v. 3. *the Ministers of God, which bear the Sword,* v. 4. In St. *Peter*, the Βασιλεύς and Ἡγεμόνες, the King, and his Governours and Magistrates, 1 *Peter* 2. 13, 14. Now there may be Kings and Emperours and Rulers, who exercise civil government without a legal Title to it, in the sense of the Objectors, yet St. *Paul* has made no Exception against them; but if they be the Powers, if they exercise the Supream Authority, they are of God, and are the Ordinance of God: for πᾶσα ἐξυσία is πᾶς ἐξυσιάζων; which evidently relates to the Exercise of Civil Authority, not to a legal Right. And why should we think the *Apostle* here intends a distinction unknown to Scripture: had there been any such Rule before given, to submit to lawful powers, but not to submit to Usurpers, there had been some pretence for understanding St. *Paul's all power* of all legal power; but there being nothing like this any where else in Scripture, if he had intended any such distinction, he ought to have said it in express words, or else no body could reasonably have understood him to intend this precept of subjection to the higher powers, only of powers that had a legal Right. For then, in order to the fulfilling of this precept, it would be necessary for Subjects to examine the Titles of Princes, and to that end to be well skill'd in the History and Laws of a Nation, and to be able to judge between a pretended and real Right, and to know exactly what gives a real Right, that they may know to whom they ought to pay subjection, and may not misplace their duty in so important a matter. And let any man judge in what perplexities this sense of the Apostles precept would involve the Consciences of men? for these are great disputes among learned men, and how then should unlearn-

The Case of the Allegiance

ed men understand them? And I cannot think that the resolution of Conscience, in such matters as all Mankind are concerned in, should depend upon such Niceties as learned men themselves cannot agree in. Especially if we consider the Case of the *Roman* Empire, in which, for so many Ages together, the Titles of their Emperours were either all of them stark nought, or the very best of them very doubtful. And yet this Epistle to the *Romans* was written to the Subjects of that Empire to direct them in the point of subjection and obedience. This I take to be little less than a demonstration, that this precept of St. *Paul* cannot be understood only of subjection to powers that had a legal Right.

Besides this, the reason the *Apostle* gives for submission to the higher powers is not a legal Right, but the Authority of God; *that all power* (or every one, who exerciseth the supreme power) *is of God*, and *the Ordinance of God*, which seems plainly intended to wave the dispute about the legality of the powers, which was the Objection of the *Pharisees*, against submission to the *Roman* power; and an Objection which no body made but themselves: they thought they were not bound by God to submit to the *Roman* powers; nay, that they were bound by the Law of God not to submit to them, as being unjust Usurpations upon the priviledges and liberties of God's people, and therefore the *Apostle* tells them, that *all power is of God*; *the powers that be are ordained of God*, wherein certainly he never intended to justifie all the *Roman* Usurpations, or to vindicate the legality of their power, which will as reasonably justifie all the Revolutions that ever were in the world; but to assert the providence of God, and his supream authority, in transferring Kingdoms and Empires, in removing Kings, and setting up Kings. And when the *Apostle* says, *All power is of God*, there is no reason to confine this to all legal powers, unless it were evidently the Doctrine of Scripture, that *usurped powers are not of God*, which is so far from being true, that the contrary is evident; *that the most high ruleth in the kingdom of men, and giveth it to whomsoever he will*, 4 *Dan.* 17. which is spoke with reference to the *four Monarchies*, which were all as manifest Usurpations as ever were in the world, and yet set up by the decree and counsel of God, and foretold by a prophetick Spirit: and whoever will confine the power and authority of God, *in changing Times and Seasons, in removing Kings and setting up Kings*, to Human Laws, ought not to be disputed with.

To

due to Soveraign Powers, &c.

To this I add, that this distinction, that only Legal, not Usurped Powers, are of God, had made the *Apostles* direction signifie nothing, for the great Question had been still undetermined, what Powers are of God, and what Powers they must obey, if some Powers be of God, and some not. When he says, *the Powers that be*, had he confined this to *the then present Powers*, it would have directed them at that time, but had been no general direction to Christians in other Ages, to obey the present powers, and then we have no direction in Scripture, what to do in such disputed Cases, unless by a parity of Reason; and if we must obey such powers, as the *Roman* power was, I know very few powers that we may not obey: for whatever Legal Right the *Roman* Emperors had, who by fear, or flattery, or other arts, extorted some kind of consent from the *Senate*, it is plain, the *Romans* themselves were great Usurpers, and had no other Right to the greatest part of their Empire, but Conquest and Usurpation.

This I'm sure, the only direction of Scripture is to submit to those who are in Authority, who are in the actual administration of Government, to reverence and obey them, to pray for them, to pay Tribute to them, *as God's Ministers, attending continually upon this very thing*, and not to resist them; but there is not the least notice given us of any kind of Duty owing or to be paid to a Prince out of Authority, and removed from the administration of Government, whatever his Right may be: We have no Example in Scripture, that any people were ever blamed for submitting to the present powers, whatever the Usurpation were, though we have Examples of their being condemned for refusing to submit to them; witness the Prophesies of *Jeremiah*, and the Discourses of our *Saviour* with the *Scribes* and *Pharisees* about paying Tribute to *Cæsar*.

Our Saviour's Argument relies wholly on the possession of power, *whose Image and Superscription hath it*? And if this be a good Reason, it is good in all other cases; that we must submit to all Princes, who are possessed of the Soveraign power, and are in the full administration of Government: The Prophet *Jeremy's* Argument is Prophecy, or an express Command from God to submit to the King of *Babylon*; and there was great reason for an express Command from God at that time, because God himself had entailed the Kingdom upon *David's* Posterity, and therefore without an express Command from God, they could not subject themselves to any other Prince, while any of that Family were living, which

is

22 *The Case of the Allegiance*
which is the reason that *Jehoiada* the High-Priest gives for deposing *Athaliah,* who had Usurped the Throne for six years, and anointing *Joash* the King's Son; *behold the King's Son shall Reign, as the Lord hath said of the Sons of David:* But where God has made no entail of the Crown, but the entail is only by Humane Laws, there is no need of Prophecy to direct people to submit to any new Prince, whom God sets over them.

For we must observe, that this was at the beginning of the *four Monarchies,* which God intended successively to erect, to whom he gave the Kingdoms of the World, not excepting his own people *Israel*; and in that Command he gave to them to submit to those Powers, (which was renewed by Christ and his Apostles) has taught all Christians to do so too, and not to oppose any Humane Right or Interest against the Divine will and pleasure, when it is sufficiently declared by the events of Providence. And the Prophecy of the *four Monarchies* is not yet at an end; for under the *fourth* Monarchy the Kingdom of *Christ* was to be set up, and *Antichrist* was to appear, and the increase and destruction of the Kingdom of *Antichrist* is to be accomplished by great Changes and Revolutions in Humane Governments; and when God has declared, that he will change Times and Seasons, remove Kings, and set up Kings, to accomplish his own wise Counsels, it justifies our necessary, and therefore innocent compliances with such Revolutions, as much as if we were expresly commanded to do so, as the *Jews* were by the *Prophet Jeremiah.* This a man may say without Enthusiasm, or pretending to understand all the Prophesies of the *Revelations,* and to apply them to their particular events, for without that we certainly know, that all the great Revolutions of the World are intended by God to serve those great ends; and when God will overturn Kingdoms and Empires, remove and set up Kings, as he sees will best serve the accomplishment of his own Counsels and Decrees, it is very hard, if Subjects must not quietly submit to such Revolutions: we must not contrary to our sworn Duty and Allegiance promote such Revolutions, upon a pretence of fulfilling Prophesies, but when they are made and setled, we ought to submit to them.

Now when we have no direction in Scripture at all about making or unmaking Kings, or restoring a dispossessed Prince to his Throne again, and all the Commands we have in Scripture about Obedience and Subjection to Government, manifestly
respect

respect the present Ruling Powers, without any distinction between Rightful or Usurped powers, it seems plainly to determine this Question on the side of the present powers; at least it leaves us to the guidance and conduct of Reason in this matter, and therefore let us impartially consider what Reason says.

2. I observe then in the next place, that this gives the easiest and most intelligible account of the Original of Humane Government; that all Power is from God, who is the Soveraign Lord of the World.

This has been a very perplext and intricate Dispute both in Religion and Politicks, and men have zealously espoused different *Hypotheses*, as they have had different ends to serve.

The matter of Fact, how Monarchies first began, and what was the Original of particular Monarchies, is very obscure for want of History, which is the only way to know it: Some think, all power was originally derived from the Choice and Consent of the People: others ascribe it to the Right of Conquest, which they think without more ado confers a Right of Government; others think Conquest gives no Right, but the Submission of the conquered people, or the long continuance of such an Usurpation does; especially when such a Government descends from Father to Son, and is become an Inheritance, either by Præscription, or Laws; which some men think then so Sacred, that they must in no case submit to any other Government, while any Legal Heir to the Crown is living, and makes his Claim.

Now I think there is no doubt, but several Governments have been begun all these ways, but still it is God, who by his Providence advances men to the Throne, and invests them with his Authority by all these ways; for the Authority is Gods, and it is his advancing them to the Throne which gives them this Authority.

It is evident, there is no Natural Authority, but the *Paternal* and *Patriarchal* Authority; and that Monarchies were erected upon the ruins or great diminution of it; and whether this were by consent, or (as is most probable) by violent Usurpations, of which *Nimrod* seems to have set the first Example, it was equally unjust; for no Authority is so Sacred, as what is Natural, which no man had Authority to give away, or to Usurp:

But

But by this means God erected Monarchies, and gave his Authority to Men, who had no Authority of their own.

If the Choice and Consent of the people makes a Prince, then no man is a Subject, but he who consents to be so; for the Major Vote cannot include my consent, unless I please; that is the effect of Law and Compact or Force, not of Nature. If Subjects give their Prince Authority, they may take it away again, if they please; there can be no irresistible Authority derived from the people; for if the Authority be wholly derived from them, who shall hinder them from taking it away, when they see fit? Upon these Principles, there can be no Hereditary Monarchy; one Generation can only choose for themselves, their Posterity having as much Right to choose as they had:

If Conquest gives a Right, then Force, the most unjust and violent Force, is Right; and then every man by the same Rule, who is stronger than I am, has a Natural Right to govern me.

Submission is only a forced and after-consent not to make a King, but to own him, who has made himself King, and whom very often we would disown and reject, were it safe to do so; and what Right can that give more than Force?

The continuance of an Usurpation can never give a Right, unless that which is wrong can grow right by continuance: An Usurper by long continuance may out-live those, who formerly wore the Crown; but does it give Right to him, who has none, that he out-lives those, who had the Right? For though no body else has any Right to the Crown, how does this make him a Rightful King, who has no Right?

An *Hereditary Right* is either a continued Usurpation, which can give no Right, or a Right by Law; that is, by the consent of the people to entail the Crown on such a Family, which, as I observed before, if Right be resolved into the Choice and Consent of the people, cannot be done; for what Right had my Ancestors three or four hundred years ago, to choose a King for me?

So that I cannot see where to fix the Foundation of Government, but in the Providence of God, who either by the choice of the major or stronger part of the people, or by Conquest, or by Submission, and the long successive continuance of power, or by Humane Laws, gives a Prince and his Family possession of the Throne, which is a good Title against all Humane Claims, and requires the Obedience and Submission of Subjects as long as God is pleased to continue him and his Family in the Throne; but it is no Title against God, if he please to advance another Prince. To

due to Sovereign Powers, &c.

To say that God sets up no Prince, who ascends the Throne without a Human and Legal Right, is to say, that some Kings are removed, and others set up, but not by God; which is a direct contradiction to Scripture; it is to say, That the *Four Monarchies* were not set up by God, because they all began by Violence and Usurpation: It is to say, That God, as well as men, is confined by Human Laws, in making Kings: It is to say, That the Right of Government is not derived from God, without the consent of the People; for if God can't make a King without the People, or against their Consent declared by their Laws, the Authority must be derived from the People, not from God; or at least if it be God's Authority, yet God can't give it himself without the People, nor otherwise than as they have directed him by their Laws.

This is all very absurd, and what those persons abhor the thoughts of, who insist so much upon a Legal Right, that they will own no King, who ascends the Throne, without it, nor believe that God places him there without and against a Legal Right: but if they would examine themselves for what Reason they believe that a King who has no Right to the Throne, is not set up by God, and invested with his Authority, they will find, That it must ultimately resolve it self into the Authority of the People to make Kings, which it is unjust for God himself to over-rule and alter; for a Legal Entail is nothing more than the Authority of the People; and if the People have such an uncontroulable Authority in making Kings, I doubt they will challenge as much Authority to unmake them too. If the sole Authority of Government be from God, and God gives this Authority only by placing a Prince in the Throne, then by whatever means he does it, it is the same thing. When such a Prince is setled in the Throne, he is God's King and Minister, and must be Reverenced and Obeyed by the People who live under his Government; thus it must be, *if all Power be of God.*

But there are several Objections against this, which must be briefly answered.

1. It is objected, That this makes a Prince lose his Right by being notoriously injured; for if a prosperous Usurper gets into the Throne, and settles himself there, God has taken away his Crown, and given it to another; and therefore he ought not to attempt the recovery of his Throne (nor any other Prince to assist him in it) which is to oppose God, and to challenge that which he has no longer any Right to.

Object.

I answer,

The Case of the Allegiance

Answer. I answer, By no means: The Providence of God removes Kings and sets up Kings, but alters no Legal Rights, nor forbids those who are dispossessed of them, to recover their Right, when they can. While such a Prince is in the Throne, it is a declaration of God's Will, that he shall Reign for some time, longer or shorter, as God pleases; and that is an obligation to Subjects to submit and obey; for Submission is owing only to God's Authority; but that one Prince is at present placed in the Throne, and the other removed out of it, does not prove, that it is God's Will it should always be so, and therefore does not divest the dispossest Prince of his Legal Right and Claim, nor forbid him to endeavour to recover his Throne, nor forbid those who are under no obligation to the Prince in possession, to assist the dispossessed Prince to recover his Legal Right: A Legal and Successive Right is the ordinary way whereby the Providence of God advances Princes to any Hereditary Throne: And this bars all other human Claims; but yet God may give the Throne to another, if he pleases; and this does not destroy the Legal Right of the dispossessed Prince, nor hinder him from claiming it, when he finds his opportunity.

But it may perhaps be farther said, If the dispossessed Prince may still have the Legal Right and Claim to the Crown, and he who is possessed of the Crown, may have none, is it not very unjust in Subjects to pay Allegiance to him who is possessed of the Throne without Right, and to withdraw their Allegiance from him who has the Right? Is not this to justifie and support Injustice and Violence, and to oppress oppressed Innocence and Right? And can the Providence of God make that our Duty, which is so manifestly unjust and wicked?

I answer; To deny any man, much more a Prince, what is his just Right, and which I am bound to give him, is certainly very unjust, and that which the Providence of God can never justifie; but then we must consider, What the Prince's Right is; and, What is the Duty of Subjects; and, When Subjects may be said to deny their Prince's Right.

The Right of the Prince is to administer the Government of the Nation; the Duty of Subjects is to submit to his Government, and obey his Laws, when he does actually administer the Government; and those who do not refuse to obey him when he governs, deny him no Right that they owe him; for there is no Duty Subjects owe to Princes, as Subjects, but to obey them; and not to obey, when they don't and can't Govern, is to deny no Right. Yes,

Yes, you'l fay, The poffeffion of the Crown, and the actual Adminiftration of Government, is his Right; and if we own any other Governing Power, we deny him that Right.

I anfwer, Suppofe he have a Legal Right to Govern, but can't; Obedience is not his Right; and therefore to pay my Obedience to thofe who do Govern, is no denial of his Legal Right; but a due Submiffion to the Providence of God, who hath a Right fuperiour to all Human Rights, in the difpofal of Crowns and Kingdoms.

The Duty of Subjects as fuch, is to obey their Prince, and fubmit to him whilft he governs, and is in poffeffion of the Throne: But then Kings muft take fome care alfo to preferve their Crowns by good Government; and if they will run the hazard of their Crowns, thofe of their Subjects are certainly not to be blamed by fuch a Prince, who did nothing to take his Crown from him.

But fome it may be will fay, That fuch Subjects are bound even in fuch a cafe to maintain and defend their King in his Throne.

I am not fo very fure of that; but this I am fure of, That whenever People have a good King, it is both their Duty and Intereft to defend him; and if they be not mifled by the Cunning and Artifice of ill men, they will certainly do fo. But if they have a very bad one, that notorioufly violates their Rights, and breaks the Conftitution upon which himfelf ftands, and ftrikes at the deareft things they have, their Religion eftablifhed by Law, and their Properties, I doubt the cafe may be altered; and though every body will not fpeak it out, yet moft may fay in their hearts, Let him go, if he cannot defend himfelf. It is enough in confcience patiently to bear fo bad a Prince, but a little too much to venture their Lives and Fortunes to keep him in the Throne to opprefs them; this is againft Reafon and Nature, and I know no Law of God which requires it: A Subject, and a Soldier; to Obey a Prince, and to Fight for him, are two things; and to be a Subject of any Prince, does not either by the Laws of God or Man, neceffarily make him a Soldier.

But have we not fworn to the King, his Heirs and Lawful Succeffors, to defend and maintain his Perfon, Crown, and Dignity? And are we not bound by this Oath?

I anfwer, 1. I grant it is fo; but then we muft diftinguifh two parts in this Oath: 1. The Natural Duty of Subjects, which is Faith and true Allegiance, or Obedience and Submiffion to the Government of the King. 2. That Duty and Obligation which is fuperinduced

ced by Law, to maintain and defend the King's Right to the Crown, and all the Dignities and Prerogatives of it, which is now made a part, not of our Natural, but Legal Allegiance.

The reason of the thing tells us, That this is not an Arbitrary, but real Distinction; and then, tho our Natual and Legal Allegiance be both included in the same Oath, they are of a distinct Consideration.

Natural Allegiance, or Obedience and Subjection to Government, is due to the King, considered in the actual Administration of Government, and no otherwise, because it can be paid only to the Regnant Prince; and it is due to all Kings, who are setled in the Government; for it is due to Government, and for that reason, to the Prince who governs.

Legal Allegiance, or Maintenance and Defence, is due only by Law, and therefore can oblige no further than Human Laws do, which must always give way to the Laws of God; and therefore Natural Allegiance (in case of a Competition) vacates the Obligation of Legal Allegiance and Oaths; as the Laws of God and Nature must take place of all humane positive Laws and Oaths. If then, I have sworn to maintain and defend my King, who has a Legal Right to the Throne, whatever is meant by this Maintenance and Defence, if he happen to be dispossessed of his Throne, and another Prince placed there, whom, in Reverence to the Authority of God, I am to obey, and submit to, without Resistance; I am absolved from my Legal Allegiance to maintain and defend my ejected Prince, because I cannot do it without violating that Allegiance, which by the Laws of God I owe to the Regnant Prince; for I cannot defend the dispossessed Prince, whom I have sworn to defend, without opposing and resisting the Regnant Prince, whom by the Laws of God I am bound to obey.

2. This Legal Allegiance, *or Maintenance and Defence*, is Sworn only to a King in Possession, and signifies no more, than to maintain and defend him in the Possession of the Throne, as having a Legal Right to it: We can legally take this Oath only to a King, who is in Possession, for it must be administred by his Authority; and the Obligation of Oaths must not be extended beyond the necessary Signification of Words; now to maintain and defend the King's Person, Crown, and Dignity, and to restore him to his Throne, when he is dispossessed, are two very different things; and therefore he, who Swears to maintain and defend, is not by virtue

of

due to Sovereign Powers, &c.   29

of that Oath obliged to reftore; while a Prince is on the Throne, Subjects are in a capacity to defend and preferve him there; and therefore may oblige themfelves to it, and there may be Reafons why this fhould be exacted from them; but in ordinary Cafes, if they cannot defend the King in Poffeffion, there is little likelihood they fhould be able to reftore him; and therefore no reafon, that Subjects fhould bind themfelves by fuch an Oath.

To venture our Lives and Fortunes to preferve the King's Perfon and Government, while he is in Poffeffion, is reafonable enough; becaufe it is a real Service to our King and Country, to prevent unjuft Ufurpations, which overturn the Government, and often unfettle or deftroy the Laws, and with them the Rights and Liberties of Subjects, as well as the Right of the King; but to Swear to do our utmoft to reftore the King, when he is difpoffeffed, is to Swear never to fubmit to ufurped Powers, but to take all Opportunities to overthrow fuch Governments to reftore our King, which is contrary to our Duty, when God removes one King, and fets up another; which expofes our Lives and Fortunes to ruin, when we cannot ferve our King by it; which provokes fuch new Powers, if they be not more merciful, to fecure themfelves by rooting out fuch fworn Enemies to their Government; and then the Confequence of this Oath, is, That if our King be driven out of the Land, we will follow him into Banifhment, or venture being hanged at home; that we will difturb all Governments, and raife Rebellions, and Civil Wars, if we can, to reftore our King, tho with the utter Ruin and Deftruction of the Nation. I believe, fhould all this be expreffed in an Oath, there is no Man in his wits would take it, for the fake of the beft Prince that ever fway'd a Scepter; and how unreafonable then is it, to expound an Oath to fuch a Senfe, as no Man would have taken it in, had it been expreffed? However it appears, that there is fuch a vaft difference between *maintaining and defending* a Regnant Prince, and *reftoring* a Difpoffeffed Prince, that to *reftore* is not neceffarily included in *maintaining.*

But we Swear not only to the King, but to his Heirs, and Lawful Succeffors, who are not in Actual Poffeffion; and therefore that muft fignify to give them Poffeffion: Right! if the King dye poffeft of the Crown, we Swear to maintain the Succeffion, and to own the true Heir, for our King; but if the King be driven out of Poffeffion, and his Heirs with him, and another Prince poffeffed of the

Throne,

Throne, this Oath can no more oblige us to set the Banished Heir upon the Throne, than to restore the Banished King.

But by swearing to the Heirs, and *Legal* or *Lawful Successors*, we Swear not to own, or submit to any Prince, who is not the Legal Heir. That I deny; we Swear, if you please, not to make it our Act, not to set up any Prince, who is not the right Heir; and we Swear to own the right Heir, if he gets Possession; but we do not Swear not to submit to any Prince, who gets into Possession, and is setled in the Throne without a Legal Right; the words signify no such thing, no more than Maintaining and Defending, signifies Restoring.

3. I observe further, That this Maintenance and Defence, which we Swear of the King's Person and Crown, is only a Legal Maintenance and Defence; for the Law will not justify, much less does it command any illegal Defence; and therefore a Legal Oath can oblige us only to a Legal Defence.

This is true, with reference to the *Cause*; for we are not bound to defend the King against Law, or when he Subverts the Laws, and Liberties, and the Legal Established Religion of the Kingdom, by Illegal Methods. A Sovereign Prince must not be resisted by force, nor must he be assisted and defended against Law; for tho the King be unaccountable, yet his Ministers and Instruments are not; and no Man is bound to serve or defend the King in that, for which by the Law of the Land he may be hanged for a Traytor; and this in a limited Monarchy, sets Bounds to Sovereign Power; for unless Subjects will betray their own Liberties, and venture to be hanged for it, such a Prince cannot hurt them; and the late Revolution teaches us, (and all Princes ought to take warning by it) how easily a Prince is ruined, when he has forfeited the Affections, and the Legal Defence of his Subjects, by the Exercise of an Illegal and Arbitrary Power; and if the Oath of Allegiance does not oblige Subjects to defend a Prince in the Exercise of an Arbitrary Power; I think, it much less obliges them to restore such a Prince, and Arbitrary Power with him.

But that which I mean by a Legal Defence, (let the Cause be what it will) is such a Defence, as the Law requires all Subjects to give their King; for a Legal Oath can require no other Defence than the Law requires.

Now the only Legal Defence, wherein all Subjects are concern'd, is either the *Militia*, or the *Posse Comitatus*, which are in the Power

of

due to Sovereign Powers, &c.

of the Regnant Prince, and cannot defend a Prince who is out of Poffeffion; and therefore, if this Oath means only a Legal Defence, it muſt be confined to the King while he is in Poffeffion, and has the Power of the Kingdom in his hands; for I cannot defend a Difpoffeffed Prince by ferving in the *Militia*, or *Poſſè Comitatus*, which is always in the Power of the Regnant Prince.

But a Prince may raife an *Army* for his Defence, befides the *Militia* of the Country; and this he may do, when he is out of Poffeffion, and Loyal Subjects ought chearfully to ferve him in it.

Now here is a great Queftion, which I am not Lawyer enough to decide; Whether a Commiffion granted by a King out of Poffeffion, be a Legal Commiffion; but be that how it will, I am fure, there is no Law that requires all Subjects to receive Commiffions from the King, tho he be in Poffeffion of the Government, nor to Lift themfelves Soldiers in his Army; and therefore this is no part of that Legal Defence which we Swear. All that Legal Defence which we Swear to the King, can be paid only to the King in Poffeffion; and what we have not Swore, we are not bound to by the Oath of Allegiance, which is the only thing we are now inquiring after. This the whole Nation, both Prince and People have, fufficiently acknowledged, by making and receiving Addreffes of *Lives and Fortunes*, which is fuppofed to fignify fome other defence than the Oath of Allegiance obliged them to; and therefore, were not of the mind of thofe Men, who think their Sworn Allegiance binds them to reſtore the King, when Difpoffeffed of his Throne, at the Expence of their Lives and Fortunes.

4. It is worth confidering alfo; That the Oath of Allegiance is a National Oath, and therefore the defence or maintenance we fwear, is National, that is, to join with our Fellow-fubjects in defending the King's Perfon and Crown: for fingle Subjects cannot do this by themfelves, and the way to oblige them all, is to impofe a National Oath to be taken by all Subjects.

Now fuch Oaths as thefe oblige every particular Man to do no injury to the King's Perfon or Crown, not to enter into Plots and Confpiracies againſt him; and as for actual defence, chearfully to venture his Life and Fortunes with his Fellow-fubjects to preferve the King. But in cafe the great Body of the Nation abfolve themfelves from thefe Oaths, and depofe their King, and drive him out of his Kingdom, and fet up another Prince in his room, it is worth considering, Whether some private men, it may be but a little handful, are still bound by their Oath, to make some weak and dangerous attempts, and to fight for their King against their Country; certainly this was not the intention of the Oath, for it is a National, not a private Defence, we swear; and therefore a general revolt of a Nation, though it should be wicked and unjustifiable, yet it seems to excuse those, who had neither hand nor heart in it, from their sworn defence of the King's Person, and Crown, and to make their compliance with the National Government innocent and necessary. For an Oath to fight for the King, does not oblige us to fight against our Country, which is as unnatural, as to fight against our King. The sum is this; God, when he sees fit, can remove Kings, or set up Kings, without any regard to human Right, as being the Sovereign Lord of the World, who rules in the Kingdoms of Men, and giveth them to whomsoever he will: but subjects, in setting up, or removing Kings, must have regard to Legal Right; and if they pull down a rightful King, and set up a King without right, (unless the Constitution of the Government in some Cases should allow it) greatly sin in it, especially when they have sworn the defence of the Legal Right, and Legal Succession: but the Duty and Allegiance of Subjects does not immediately respect Right, but the actual administration of Government, when there is a setled Government in a Nation; for that is God's Authority, which must be obeyed: no man must swear away this, no more than any other part of his Duty; and no man does swear away this by the Oath of Allegiance, as I have already shown.

Objection. But it will be farther objected, That if this Doctrine do not take away the Legal Right, yet it makes it impossible for such an injur'd Prince to recover his Right, when all his Subjects have sworn Allegiance to a new Prince, and therefore can no longer assist him.

Answer. I answer; This may be called a difficulty in Providence, if you please, but it is no difficulty to the Subject, if he pursue his Duty in it, unless a passionate affection for the dispossessed Prince make it a difficulty: but such a misfortune as this, can rarely happen to a beloved Prince; and when Subjects are overpowered by force, and can neither defend themselves, nor their Prince, there is no remedy left but to yield to necessity, and leave every thing else to the Divine Providence.

The Divine Providence has ways and methods of removing Kings, and setting up Kings, which we are not aware of, nor concerned

due to Sovereign Powers, &c.

to know, because it is no part of our duty: No man could have foreseen, how *Ch.* II. should have returned, who had a powerful Army against him; or *J.* II. be driven out of his Kingdom, at the Head of a powerful Army, without shedding of blood. All the Plots and Conspiracies of the Loyal Party were vain, and had no other effect, but to bring some worthy and gallant Men to an unhappy end; but what they could not do, God did without them; and all such Cases we must leave to God.

But does not this encourage daring and ambitious Spirits to grasp *Objection.* at Crowns, and invade their Neighbours, when they know that Success gives them Sovereign Authority, and obliges Subjects, notwithstanding all former Oaths, to pay all Duty and Allegiance to them?

Ambitious and daring Spirits need no other encouragement but *Answer.* Power to grasp at Crowns; and if they have this, they value no more: promise them but Success, and they will try, whether Subjects will obey or not. I dare say, such men never took it into consideration, whether Subjects would think themselves bound in Conscience to obey them, in case they prevailed; they seldom trouble themselves about Conscience, but trust to other Arguments to secure their Thrones, when they have once gotten them. And if they take this Doctrine all together, as they must do, if they encourage their Ambition, by Reason, and Principles, it will give no encouragement to Ambitious Spirits without a great dose of Enthusiasm: For if the Kingdoms of the World be disposed by God, and no Art or Power can place any Prince on the Throne, but by God's appointment, unless they can flatter themselves, that God has ordain'd them to be Kings, it will check all their ambitious Attempts, which God can so easily defeat.

But if this Doctrine should prove inconvenient to Princes, and dangerous to their Thrones; I am sure the contrary Doctrine is much more dangerous to Subjects, when any such Revolution happens; for it sacrifices them to the rage and fury of Conquering and Reigning Princes, when they are obliged by Principles of Conscience to oppose and disown their Government, which it is folly to think any Prince will endure; and though I have as great a reverence for Princes as any man, I do not think the Right and Interest of any Prince so considerable, as the Safety and Preservation of a Nation, and the Lives and Fortunes of all his Subjects.

F   In

The Case of the Allegiance

In a word, The Objectors do not think it a sufficient Confutation of the Doctrine of Non-resistance, and Passive Obedience, to say, That this puts it into the King's power, to invade the Laws and Liberties, the Lives and Fortunes, of his Subjects at pleasure; and yet there is more danger of this from an Ambitious and Arbitrary Prince, than there is, that the Doctrine of Obedience and Submission to the Governing Powers, should encourage Ambitious Spirits to invade their Neighbours Thrones; the Divine Providence takes care of all such extraordinary Cases, and there we must leave them.

Object. But have not Pyrates and Robbers as good a Title to my Purse, as an Usurper has to the Crown, which he seizes by as manifest force and violence? Does not the Providence of God order and dispose all these events? And are we not bound then as much to submit to Pyrates, as to Usurpers?

Answ. The dispute is not about human and legal Right in either Case, but about Authority, which is the only reason of a conscientious subjection; now no Man pretends, that Thieves and Pyrates have God's Authority, to which we must submit; but the Scripture expresly tells us, That Kingdoms are disposed by God; That all Power is of God; and therefore when any Prince, by what unjust means soever, with respect to Men, is placed in the Throne, and setled there, He is advanc'd by God, is God's Ordinance, God's Minister, and must be obeyed for Conscience sake: And therefore the outrages of Thieves and Pyrates are very impertinently alledged in this Cause. They have force and violence, which every Man must submit to, when he cannot help it; but Soveraign Power is God's Authority, though Princes may be advanced to it by no honester means, than Thieves take a Purse, or break open my House, and take my Money, or Goods. The beginnings of the four Monarchies were no better, and yet their Power was God's.

Object. But did not *Jehojada* the High-priest anoint *Joash* the King's Son, and depose and kill *Athaliah*, who had usurped the Throne for six
2 Chr. 23. years? And did he think then, that an Usurper's possession of the
1, 2. Throne, required the Allegiance and Fidelity and Obedience of the Subject?

Answ. 1. All that this Story amounts to, is no more than this, That when the Legal and Rightful Heir is actually possessed of his Throne, Subjects may return to their Allegiance, and by the Authority of their King prosecute the Usurper; for *Joash* was first anointed and
pro-

due to Sovereign Powers, &c.

proclaimed, before any one stirred a finger against *Athaliah*: Now this is a very different Case from raising Rebellions against a Prince, who is in the possession of the Throne, to restore an ejected Prince.

2. But this was a peculiar Case; for God himself had entailed the Kingdom of *Judah* on the posterity of *David*, and therefore nothing could justify their submission to an Usurper, when the King's Son was found, to whom the Kingdom did belong by a Divine entail; and by this, *Jehojada* justifies what he did, *Behold, the King's son shall reign, as the Lord hath said of the sons of David.* Now when God has entailed the Crown by an express declaration of his Will, and nomination of the Person, or Family, that shall Reign (as it was in the Kingdom of *Judah*) Subjects are bound to adhere to their Prince of God's chusing, when he is known, and to persecute all Usurpers to the utmost, and never submit to their Government; but in other Kingdoms, where God makes Kings, and entails the Crown, not by express nomination, but by his Providence, the placing a Prince in the Throne, and setling him there in the full administration of the Government, is a reason to submit to him, as to God's Ordinance and Minister.

But it is further urged, That according to these Principles, all Kings are set up by God, and yet God expresly charges *Israel* with making Kings without him, *Hosea* 8. 4. *They have set up Kings, but not by me; they have made Princes, and I knew it not.*

Now 1. This is not true as to all the Kings of *Israel*, after their separation from the Tribe of *Judah*; for some of the Kings were set up by God's own appointment and nomination, as *Jeroboam* and *Jehu*, and their posterity: So that this can be true only of those Kings, who Reigned over *Israel* between the Posterity of *Jeroboam* and *Jehu*, and after the Kingdom was taken from the Line of *Jehu*.

2. One of these Kings was *Baashah*, who slew *Nadab* the Son of *Jeroboam*, and made himself King without God's express nomination and appointment, and yet God tells him, *I exalted thee out of the dust, and made thee Prince over my people Israel.* And all the other Kings, who were not nominated by God, nor anointed by any Prophet, no more than *Baasha* was, were yet set up by God, as he was.

3. The true Answer then is this: *Israel* was originally a *Theocracy*, as well as *Judah*; and though God allowed them at their request

V. 3

Object.

Answ.

1 Kings 15. 27. 16. 2.

to have Kings, yet he reserved the appointment of them to himself; and therefore, as in the Kingdom of *Judah*, he entailed the Crown on *David*'s Posterity, so he appointed *Jeroboam* to be the first King in *Israel*, and they ought, when that Line was cut off, to have consulted God, and received his nomination, by his Prophets, of a new King; but instead of that, when *Jeroboam*'s Line, and *Jehu*'s, were cut off, who were the only Kings named by God, and anointed by his Prophets, they submitted to any, who could set themselves over them: This was a great fault in a people who were under the immediate Government of God; for hereby they fell out of the state of *Theocracy*, into the common condition of the rest of the World, where Kings are set up by the Providence of God, as *Baasha* was, but not by his appointment and nomination; which was the privilege of *Israel*, but which it seems they despised and neglected, as no privilege or favour; as great a Crime, as for *Esau* to contemn his Birth-right; and therefore are very justly reproved for it by God, and charged with it as a great crime, it being in effect, a renouncing their prerogative, of being God's peculiar People.

3*dly*, To justify this Doctrine of Obedience and Allegiance to the present Powers, there is an Argument, which I know some Men will not like, but must be a good Argument to those, who most scruple the new Oath; *viz.* That it is founded on the same Principle with the Doctrine of *Non-resistance* and *Passive-obedience*, and therefore both must be true, or both false; for it is founded on this Principle, That God makes Kings, and invests them with his Authority; which equally proves, That all Kings, who have received a Soveraign Authority from God, and are in the actual administration of it (which is the only evidence we have that they have received it from God) must be obeyed, and must not be resisted. Set aside this Principle, That all Soveraign Princes receive their Authority from God, and I grant that Non-resistance is nonsense; for there is no other irresistible Authority, but that of God. If God have given a Soveraign Authority to them, they are immediately his Ministers, and unaccountable to their Subjects; but if they receive their Authority from Men, and human Laws, I cannot imagine, that their Power is any more than a Trust, of which they must give an account to those who have entrusted them with it, according to those Laws, by which they were entrusted to exercise that Power; for whether there be any express provision made in the Law to call them

due to Sovereign Powers, &c.

them to an account or not, the nature of the thing proves, that if they receive their Power from Men, they are accountable to them; for those who give Power, may take an account of the use and abuse of it.

I am sure St. *Paul*, who most expresly teaches this Doctrine of Rom. 13. Non-resistance, joyns these two together, Obedience to the present Powers, and Non-resistance, and deduces them both from the same Principle, That all Power is of God: *Let every soul be subject to the higher powers, for all power is of God; the powers that be, are ordained of God; he therefore that resisteth the power, resisteth the ordinance of God, and they that resist, shall receive to themselves damnation.*

And Bp. *Overal*'s *Convocation Book*, which is lately published, the principal design of which is to assert the irresistible Authority of Sovereign Princes, does as plainly assert this too, That all setled Governments, whatever their beginnings were, have God's Authority, and must be obeyed; of which, more above: For those wise Men, who sate in that *Convocation*, plainly saw the necessary connexion between Non-resistance, and Obedience to the present Powers; both which were equally resolved into the Authority of God, in removing Kings, and setting up Kings. So that Obedience and Allegiance to the present Powers, when they are once well setled among us, is so far from being a renouncing of the Doctrine of Non-resistance and Passive-obedience, that those who refuse to comply, must renounce the only Principle whereon that Doctrine is reasonably founded, and consequentially renounce the Doctrine it self.

4*thly*, To say, That when the Divine Providence has removed one King, and set up another, we must not own this new Prince, nor pay the Duty of Subjects to him, if he have no Legal Right, is to deny God's Authority to remove Kings, or to set up Kings against Human Law; for he cannot make a King, if he cannot oblige us to obey him; nor can he remove a King, if he cannot discharge us from our Allegiance to him; and those are bold men who will venture to say, in plain contradiction to Scripture, that God cannot remove or set up Kings.

5*thly*. Nay this limits the Providence of God, in governing Kings, and protecting Innocent and Injured Subjects: We say, the Punishment of Sovereign Princes, who are unaccountable to their Subjects, is peculiar to God, who is the King of kings; and thus we answer the Objections against Non-Resistance, That if Princes abuse their

Power,

Power, God will punish them for it, and deliver their oppressed Subjects; but it seems God has no way to do this, but either to turn their hearts, or to take them out of the World; for he cannot remove them from the Throne; or if he does, the Subjects are never the better for it; for they must not own any other Prince, though he would be never so kind to them; but must bring new calamities upon themselves by an obstinate adhering to their old Prince, and provoking the new one: This seems very hard, that when God has actually delivered us, we must refuse our deliverance; That we will not allow God to deliver us, unless he do it by Law; as if God were as much confined to human Laws, as Men are: It is enough, methinks, if we suffer patiently, without violating the Laws to deliver our selves; but let God who is above all human Laws, deliver us what way he pleases.

6thly, That which is still more considerable, is the necessity of Government to preserve human Societies; for human Societies must not dissolve into a *Mob*, or Mr. *Hobbs*'s state of Nature, because the Legal Prince has lost his Throne, and can no longer govern. Bishop *Sanderson* tells us, That the end of Civil Covernment, and of that Obedience which is due to it, is the Safety and Tranquility of Human Societies; and therefore whatever is necessary and useful to this end, becomes our Duty; for the End prescribes the Means.

Quicquid enim finis alicujus gratia faciendum est, eatenus fieri oportet, in quantum ei fini consequendo necessarium vel utile videbitur. Civilis autem regiminis, ejusque quæ ipsi debita est obedientiâ, finis est, humanæ Societatis salus & tranquilitas. De Oblig. Consc. Præl. 5. Sect. 19.

And therefore this Great Man, and the most zealous *Loyalists*, do own it lawful for Subjects to pay some kind of submission, and compliance, to Usurped Powers. Let us then examine what it is they allow, and whether it answers the great End, which gives Law in all these Cases, The safety and tranquility of Human Societies.

Ibid. Sect. 16, 17, 18, 19.

They grant then, that we may obey the Laws of such a Prince, who has no Right or Authority to make them, if they contain nothing which is sinful (which is an exception against all Laws, whatever Prince makes them) and may defend our Countrey against a Foreign Enemy, may administer Justice to reward the Good, and punish the Wicked, and preserve the Trade and Commerce of the Nation: but then we must have no regard to the Authority of the Prince, nor of his Laws; for he has no Authority, and his Laws do not oblige the Conscience; but we may thus far comply to preserve
our

due to Sovereign Powers, &c. 39

our felves, our Lives, and Fortunes, and Eftates, and for the good of the Community, and out of gratitude to the Reigning Prince for his protection, and the many Bleffings they enjoy under his Government; though a late *Writer* thinks this gratitude a little too much, and not owing to an *Ufurper*; which feems ftrange; for I will thank any man, and make grateful Returns too of his kindnefs, who has power (whatever his Authority be) to do me hurt, and does me none, but a great deal of good. I am forry Loyalty, which is a very great Virtue, fhould put men out of conceit with any kind or inftances of Gratitude; which I think is not a lefs Virtue than that. But tho I greatly reverence the profound Judgment of Bifhop *Sanderfon*, I cannot be of his mind in this point; if the Safety and Tranquility of Human Societies requires any thing of us, it both requires and juftifies a great deal more.

For 1. As he ftates the matter, this deftroys Civil Government, and a governed Society; for here is neither King, nor Subject, no Authority to Command, nor Duty to Obey; and I fuppofe no Man, who confiders it well, will call this a Civil Government, or a Civil Society, to which Authority and Obedience is Effential: He would have a Civil Society preferved, this is the fundamental Law of all; but he will allow no Authority to fupport it, which is as vain a defign, as to refolve to maintain the Superftructure, but to take away the Foundation. The Prince governs by force without Authority; the Subject obeys for fear or gratitude, without a fenfe of Duty, which may laft as long as the Prince has Power, or the Subjects are in good Humour, and no longer, and is this a fure bottom, for the Safety and Tranquility of Human Societies? If Human Societies muft be preferved, then the neceffities of Government give Authority to the Prince, and lay an Obligation of Duty on the Subject; if God will preferve Human Societies, we muft conclude, that when he removes one King out of the Throne, he gives his Authority to him whom he places there; for without Authority, Human Societies muft disband; Power may tye them together a while, but can never unite them into a Civil Body, without the Bands and Ligaments of Duty and Confcience.

2. For I would ask, Whether the care of my own Prefervation, and the publick Duty, and Gratitude to the Government for my Protection, do oblige me in Confcience to obey and fubmit to the Government, and the Prince who Governs; and to wifh and pray for,

The Case of the Allegiance

for, and do my utmost to endeavour their Prosperity? If it does, I see no difference between this and Allegiance; and what I am bound in Counscience to do, I may swear to do: If it does not, then I am at Liberty to disturb the Government, notwithstanding all my gratitude, when I can; nay, am under Obligation by my Allegiance to the Dispossessed Prince, to do it when I can; and how does this contribute to the Safety and Tranquility of Human Societies?

3. Suppose then the Government does not think its self safe, to leave all Men at Liberty to disturb it when they please, and when they have a promising Opportunity to do it, but should require an Oath of Fidelity from them, which, we see, is the universal Practice of all Governments; what shall Subjects do in this Case?

According to these Principles, no Subject, when his Rightful Prince, to whom he owed, or to whom he had sworn Allegiance (which the Bishop makes the same Case) is dispossessed, ought to swear Fidelity and Allegiance to any other Prince; and now, then let us suppose, that they all did their Duty, and refused this Oath, and the Prince had power enough to compel them; what must be the effect of this, but the utter Ruin and Destruction of the Nation? The Land, indeed, would remain as it was, and where it was, for that can't be removed; but the People of it must either be destroyed, or imprisoned, or transplanted into some Foreign Countries, as was formerly practiced in the *Eastern* Conquests, witness the *Ten Tribes*, who were carried away Captive, and the Country new peopled; and is not this a Dissolution of Human Society? And if the Preservation of Human Society, be the great ultimate end of Government, and will justify what it makes necessary, nothing can be a Duty, which if universally observed, must unavoidably in all such Revolutions of Government, destroy Human Societies.

For to say, That it can never be supposed, that all, or the greatest part of any Kingdom in such Revolutions will adhere to their Duty, and obstinately refuse to swear Allegiance to a new Prince, and that is sufficient to preserve the Nation, tho some few conscientious People suffer by it, does not alter the Case; for still, according to these Principles, Human Societies in such Revolutions cannot be preserved without Sin; for if all Men did their Duty, they must all be destroyed. Now, I believe it will be hard to perswade

any

any confidering Men, that that which in fuch Cafes is neceffary to preferve a Nation, is a Sin; and that which will infallibly deftroy it, is a Duty and Virtue; if we allow the fafety and prefervation of Human Societies, to be the great Law of all.

4. I obferve further, that as cautious as the Bifhop is, That we fhould pay Obedience to Ufurped powers, without owning their Authority; yet he is forced to allow us to do fuch things for the publick Good, as cannot be done without owning the Authority; as the Defence of our Country againft a Foreign Enemy, and the Adminiftration of publick Juftice; for this muft be done by Commiffion from the King, and, I fuppofe, to take a Commiffion from him, owns his Authority, and owns it to be a good Authority; for if they hang any Man either by Military Difcipline, or Civil Juftice, and have not good Authority for it, they are Murderers. The truth is, to exercife all the Acts of Civil Government, which are neceffary for the Community, without owning the Authority of the Prince, in whofe Name, and by whofe Authority all is tranfacted, is a Riddle to me; if we muft not own the Authority of the Prince, we muft do nothing by his Authority, and then Civil Government in fuch Cafes muft ceafe, and Human Societies diffolve. So that the prefervation of Human Societies does of neceffity force us to own the Authority, even of *Ufurped* Powers; and if the prefervation of Human Societies be the end of Civil Government, and the reafon of that Obedience which we owe to Government, as the *Bifhop* afferts; then when an obftinate Allegiance to the Difpoffeffed Prince muft diffolve Civil Government, the reafon of that Allegiance ceafes, and therefore that Allegiance muft be at an end; and when Allegiance to Ufurped Powers, is neceffary to the prefervation of the Society, it muft become a Duty.

5. The *Bifhop* refolves all this into the prefumed Confent of the ejected Prince, that his Subjects fhould rather confult their own fafety by a modeft compliance with the prefent Powers, than bring certain Ruin upon themfelves by an unfeafonable Oppofition: Now tho I confefs, I lay no ftrefs upon a prefumed Confent; yet, if we will prefume, we fhould prefume all that is reafonable, that is, all that is neceffary for the Prefervation of his Subjects, when he can govern them, and protect them no longer; and then we may prefume his Confent to Oaths of Allegiance and Fidelity, when this is neceffary to their prefervation; and I can very eafily prefume, that Princes think this a lefs fault, than fome Subjects do; they know what

Ibid. Sect. 21.

what they themselves expect from Subjects, where they have Power, whatever their Right be, and therefore cannot complain of their Subjects, if they pay it to another Prince, in whose Power they are; this is the Practice of the whole World, and Princes know it; and may as reasonably be presumed to allow it, as any other Act of Obedience and Subjection to Usurped Powers. And tho I will not meddle with that Question, Whether a King's leaving his Kingdom in a great Fright, without any one to Govern and Protect his Subjects, be to all intents and purposes an Abdication of the Government? Yet one may reasonably presume, that a King, who forsakes his Kingdom to consult his own Safety, will give his Subjects leave to consult theirs; if this will justify a King to save himself by leaving his Kingdom; why will it not justify Subjects, when their King has left them, to submit and comply with the prevailing Powers, as far as is necessary to preserve themselves? That is, even by Oaths of Allegiance, if that be necessary: Self-preservation is as much a Law to Subjects, as to the Prince; and he is as much sworn to Govern and Protect his Subjects, as they are to Obey and Defend him; and if the necessities of Self-preservation absolve him from his Oath of governing and protecting his People; I desire to know, why the same necessity will not absolve Subjects from their Oaths to their Prince? Protection and Allegiance are not so reciprocal, as to be the necessary Conditions of each other; that if a Prince violate his Oath of Governing by Law, and instead of Protecting does Oppress his Subjects, Subjects are then freed from their Oath of Allegiance, and may take Arms against their Prince; for tho Protection and Defence are the Duties of Relatives, of a Prince and his Subjects; yet they are not necessarily such Relative Duties, as that neither of them can be performed unless both be. A Prince may govern by Law, and protect his Subjects, and yet in Fact they deny their Allegiance to him; and Subjects may pay their Allegiance to their Prince when he Oppresses them; these Duties may be distinctly and separately observed, and therefore do not in their own Nature, either infer or destroy each other. But Government and Allegiance are such Relatives, as do *mutuo se ponere & tollere*; the one cannot subsist without the other: if the Prince can't Govern, the Subject can't Obey; and therefore, as far as he quits his Government, he quits their Allegiance, and leaves his Subjects as he does his Crown, to be possessed by another, and must recover them both together.

Re

due to Sovereign Powers, &c.

He may have a Legal Right to both, but he cannot actually have the Subjects Allegiance without the Crown; nor can Subjects pay him their Allegiance, without his being restored to the Possession of his Throne, no more than they can obey, when he can't command; or submit, when he has no Power to govern; or defend his Person and Crown, when he has withdrawn his Person, and left his Crown. This is as certain as any Proposition in *Logick*; and to extend Allegiance beyond the Actual Administration of Government, is to preserve a *Relative* without its *Correlate*: for when one of the Relatives is lost, the *Relation* is destroyed, and nothing but the Memory of it left.

7thly, These Principles answer all the ends of Government, both for the security of the Prince and Subjects, and that is a good Argument to believe them true.

A Prince who is in Possession, is secured in Possession by them, (as far as any Principles can secure him) against all Attempts of his Subjects, who must reverence God's Authority in him; and submit to him without Resistance, though they are ill used.

They will not indeed serve the Revolutions of Government, to remove one King, and set up another; and if they would, Princes might be jealous of them; for whatever Service they might do them at one turn, they might do them as great Disservice at another: The Revolutions of Government are not the Subjects Duty, but God's Prerogative; and therefore it is not likely that he has prescribed any certain Rules or Methods for the overturning and changing Government, which he keeps in his own hands, and which when he sees fit to do it, he never wants ways and means of doing.

But when any Prince is setled in the Throne, by what means soever it be, these Principles put an end to all disputes of Right and Title, and bind his Subjects to him by Duty and Conscience, and a Reverence of God's Authority; which is the fastest hold he can possibly have of them; for those whom Religion will not bind, nothing but Force can.

And therefore these are the only Principles which in such Revolutions can make Government easie both to Prince and People; and if Government must be preserved in all Revolutions, those are the best Principles which are most for the ease and safety of it.

But on the other hand, such an immoveable and unalterable Allegiance, as is thought due only to a Legal Right and Title, and

G 2 must

The Case of the Allegiance

must be paid to none, but to a Legal and Rightful Prince, serves no ends of Government at all; but overturns all Government, when such a Prince is dispossessed of his Throne, how long soever he continue dispossessed: And what long *Inter-regnums* may this occasion, to the dissolution of Human Societies?

If you say that this is the best Principle to prevent all Revolutions of Government, when it is known, that Subjects are bound in Conscience not to submit to any Illegal and Usurping Powers; and this is very much for the peace and security of Human Societies; I answer,

1. If this Principle would prevent all Revolutions of Government, it is a demonstration against it, that it is a bad Principle, a meer Human Invention, which cannot come from God. For since God has reserved to himself his Sovereign Prerogative of removing Kings, and setting up Kings; since this is sometimes necessary for the preservation of the Church, and the deliverance of the Good from Oppression and Tyranny, and for the just Punishment either of King or People; it is impossible that he should give any such Laws to mankind, as shall debar him from the exercise of this Prerogative, in what way he pleases; yet it is certain God cannot make Kings, if he cannot oblige Subjects to obey them; and that he cannot do, if they must obey and submit only to Legal Kings.

2. It is evident, That this Principle was either unknown to the World before, (and that is an argument that it is not the natural sense of mankind), or else, That this Principle cannot prevent the Revolutions of Government; for there have been such Revolutions in all Ages, and I believe will be to the end of the World.

3. Since then such Revolutions will happen, such Principles as must dissolve Human Societies, when such Revolutions happen, or expose the most innocent and conscientious men to the greatest Sufferings, without serving any good end by them, cannot be true; for the end of Government is the Preservation of Human Societies, and therefore that can be no good Principle of Government, which in any turn of Affairs, if pursued, must dissolve Human Societies.

Nor can that be a true Principle, which at any time obliges honest men to lose their Lives, their Estates, their Liberties, in opposition to the Government of the Nation wherein they live, when they may preserve them all by Obedience and Submission to the Government: I am sure the Scripture teaches us to suffer patiently in Obedience

dience to Government, but not to suffer in Opposition to it: And when the very Reason of our Obedience to Government, is for the preservation of Human Societies, and that we our selves may enjoy the Blessings of Government, it seems very strange to extend this Duty to the overthrow of Human Societies, and to deny our selves the Security and the Blessings of Government; which is to extend a Duty to such cases, as contradict the only Reason, whereon that Duty is founded.

It is true, we must in all cases be contented to suffer in doing our Duty; for we must chuse rather to suffer than to sin; and it is no Argument that any thing ceases to be my Duty, because it exposes me to Suffering: But then we must be very sure that it is our Duty; that it is expresly enjoyned us by the Laws of God or Nature, before we venture to suffer for it: But when we are to learn our Duty, not from any express Law of God or Nature, but from the Reason and Nature of things, it is a sufficient Argument, that is not my Duty, which will expose me to great Sufferings, without serving any good end; nay, which exposes me to Sufferings, for contradicting the natural end and intention of that Duty, for which I pretend to suffer.

4. But let us grant that this Principle is the best Security to the Rights of Princes; is the Right of any Prince so Sacred as to stand in competition with the very being of Human Societies, and the safety and preservation of all his Subjects? And must we then defend a Prince's Right, with the destruction of the Nation, and the Ruin of all his Subjects? Which is most necessary, That the Nation should be governed, or, That such a Prince should govern it? And if he be driven out of his Kingdoms, and cannot govern, must we then have no Government? Or how shall the Nation be governed, if Subjects are bound in conscience to obey, and pay Allegiance to no other Prince? This is to make all mankind the Slaves and Properties of Princes; as if all men were made for Princes, not Princes for the government of men.

This, I think, is abundantly sufficient to justifie our Obedience and Allegiance to the present Powers, though it should at any time happen, that the Legal and Rightful Prince should lose his Throne.

But there is a great prejudice against all this; for so I call it, rather than an Objection; for there is no Argument in it, nor can it be formed into an Argument; viz. that this will equally serve all Revolutions of Government, whatever they be: Upon these Principles we might

The Case of the Allegiance

might submit and swear to a *Rump Parliament*, or to another *Protector*, or to a *Committee of Safety*, or whatever else you please: And yet under that Usurpation, the Loyal Nobility, Gentry, and Clergy, thought themselves bound in Conscience to oppose that Usurpation at their utmost peril; And shall we Arraign them all, as resisting God's Ordinance by their opposition to those Usurped Powers, and their attempts to restore their King to his Throne?

This, as I observed, is a great prejudice, but no Argument; for if these Principles be true, and according to these Principles they might have complied with those Usurpations; that they did not, is no confutation of them.

But yet, I suppose, all Men see a vast difference between these two Cases; it is evident those Loyal persons, both of the Clergy and Laity, who suffered in the former Cause, and have now complied with the present Government, think there is a vast difference between them; and must think themselves more reproached and injured by such a Comparison, than by such Principles as justify their present compliance: And the great Body of the Nobility, Gentry, and Clergy, who have sworn Allegiance to their present Majesties, would take it very ill to be thought less Loyal than those were, who suffered for King *Charles* I. and II. under those Usurpers; and therefore they also must apprehend a vast difference between these two cases.

But what is it that makes this difference? If you will allow the supposition, That the Rightful King is dispossessed; and that in such a case it is lawful to comply with any Government, which becomes the setled Government of the Nation.

I answer; The difference is very great upon all accounts; and that no man may wonder at the obstinate Loyalty of those days, and the easie and ready compliances now, (from whence some men conclude a renouncing the Principles of the old Church-of-*England*-Loyalty, to the great scandal of Religion), I shall show the difference upon many accounts; and all together will be more than answer enough.

1. First then, The great Villanies of those days, in an open and bare-fac'd Rebellion, persisted in after the most Gracious Offers and Condescentions; and in the Barbarous Murder of one of the Best Princes in the World, was enough to prejudice wise and good men, against all compliances, though they had been lawful; for who that could possibly avoid it, would submit to such men?

2. The

due to Sovereign Powers, &c.

2. The barbarous Usage the King's Friends met with, made a Submission and Compliance useless and impossible: Those who had fought for their King, or expressed any dislike of those Proceedings, whom they had any jealousie or suspicion of, or whose Estates they had a mind to possess themselves of, were plundered, sequestred, imprisoned, forced to sculk and hide at home, or flie abroad, to preserve their Lives and Liberties.

3. *Bishops*, *Deans*, and *Prebendaries* were turned out, and their Lands and Revenues sold; the Loyal Clergy were *Malignants* for what they had done; and had no way to keep their Livings, especially if they were of any Value, but by renouncing the Church of *England*, as well as by Submission to that Government, which I believe, notwithstanding their ready compliance in taking the Oaths, the Clergy at this day would more universally have refused, than they did then.

4thly, Another difficulty was, That the whole Government both of Church and State was overturned, which was the Fundamental Constitution of the Nation: The King was not only Murdered, and the Rightful Heir driven out of the Land, but the Monarchy it self was destroyed, and neither King, Lords, nor Commons, left; but a few of the House of Commons, who by Force and Power had turned the rest out of doors, undertook to govern all, in the name of the Commons of *England*; which was such an Invasion on the Rights and Liberties of their Countrey, (which are as sacred as the Rights of the King), as required the utmost opposition that could be made. And it may be, if it be well considered, the Defence of Monarchy, and the Rights and Prerogatives of the Crown, will appear a very material part of the Oath of Allegiance, which may bind Subjects when the Person of the King is changed; and may make them think themselves more obliged to restore such a Prince, when they cannot restore Monarchy, and the Ancient Laws and Government of the Nation without him.

5. And moreover it is plain, That their Government was never setled; it was frequently changed, and new modelled, which was no Argument of Settlement; and which is more than that, they had not a National Consent and Submission.

Men, who were forced, submitted to force; but the Nation did not by any National Act ever own them; for I think the *Rump-Parliament*, who were the Usurpers themselves; or some little packt *Conventicles*, rather than *Parliaments*, could not be called the *Representatives* of the Nation. This

The Case of the Allegiance

This seems to be muchlike the Case which *Bishop* Overal's *Convocation-Book* mentions in relation to *Antiochus*; who had by force kept the *Jews* in subjection for some years; and yet when *Mattathias* took Arms in defence of their Religion, they justify this Action by saying, That the Government of *Antiochus* was not setled among them, either by *Submission or Continuance*; that is, tho People were forced to submit to Power, his Government was not owned by any Publick, National Submission; and in such Cases a long continuance is required to settle a Government; whereas a National Submission settles a Government in a short time; as we may conclude from what they tell us of the Settlement of *Alexander*'s Government among the *Jews*, who was but a very little while with them; but *Jaddus* the *High-Priest*, and the Governing-part of the Nation submitting to him; this setled his Government in a few days.

This shows how unlike all this was to our present Case in every particular; that those who thought it their Duty never to submit to that wicked Usurpation, are now satisfied, they may submit with a good Conscience to their present Majesties.

In our present Case, all things are quite contrary to what they were in the former; every thing concurred to make the Nation fond of such a Change, and very easy under it.

King *James*, more, I hope, by following ill Counsels, than by his own Inclination, had effectually removed all Prejudices and Objections against such a Revolution, excepting the Obligations of Duty and Conscience.

In the late times of Rebellion and Usurpation, all the Friends of Monarchy, and of the *English* Government, and of the Church of *England*, and of the Liberties of their Country, and of their own Honours and Fortunes, were bound in Interest to take all Opportunities to restore the King. In our late Revolution, the very same Reasons and Interests disposed all Men to be very well contented to part with their King, if they had known how to do it honestly; for the Continuance of his Government, by the bold Steps, and extraordinary Methods he had taken, gave them great Apprehensions that all these were in danger, even the Rights and Prerogatives of the Crown it self (the preservation of which was a main end of the Oath of Allegiance) by his Submission to the *See* of *Rome*, and rejecting the Oath of *Supremacy*, and as far as he could, absolving his Subjects from it; and yet in that Oath alone, we Swear to the *Lawful* Successor, in Opposition to the pretences of the Bishop of *Rome*, to depose, and set up Kings at pleasure, for the Service of the Church. This

This helpt some Men easily to absolve themselves from the Obligation of their Oaths; for they could not think, that Oaths, which were made and imposed for the Preservation of a *Protestant* Prince, and the Protestant Rights and Liberties of Church and State, could oblige them to defend and maintain a Prince in his Usurpations, as they thought on both.

This made his Subjects, and even his Army desert his Service, when the Prince came with a Foreign Force; and this made it necessary for him to leave the Kingdom, and to leave his Subjects in the Hands of the Prince; which made an easie way for the Prince to be placed on the Throne.

Now not to dispute the legality of all this, here was nothing so formidable, as to prejudice an honest Man against submission and compliance, as there was in the late times of Rebellion; nothing that could reasonably hinder a compliance, but an Opinion, that we must never pay Allegiance to any but a Legal King; and possibly had that Point been waved; no Protestant would have disputed a quiet and chearful submission to the Government.

To fight against a King, and not to fight for him, I think are two very different things; and when Kings make it impossible to fight for them, without fighting against the Religion and Liberties of our Country, they may thank themselves, if their Subjects cannot defend them. This is a dangerous state Princes bring themselves into, especially where there are different Persuasions in a Nation: when some Men think, they may lawfully defend their Religion and Liberties against the Usurpations of their Prince; and others think, they are not bound to defend and maintain their Prince in his illegal Usurpations on their Religion and Liberties; for a little opposition without any defence will quickly ruin any Prince. To take a Crown from a Prince, and his Liberty and Life with it, and to suffer him to leave his Crown if he pleases, and to desert his Government, are two very different things.

I cannot indeed think (neither do I believe, that any body else does) that for a King to leave his Crown and Government in a fright is in all cases necessarily to be interpreted such an Abdication as is equivalent to a voluntary Resignation; whereby he renounces all future Right and Claim to it. But if he have reduced himself to such a state, that he is forced for his own preservation to leave his Kingdom and Government; it is plain, that in some sence he leaves his Throne vacant too; that is, there is no body in it, no body in the actual Administration of the Government.

Thus far I think Subjects may be very guiltless, who do not drive the King away, but only suffer him quietly to escape out of his Kingdoms; for this is no *Rebellion*, no *Resistance*, but only *Non-Assistance*, which may be very innocent: for there are some cases, wherein Subjects are not bound to assist their Prince; and if ever there were such a case, this was it.

What then shall Subjects do, when the King is gone, and the Government Dissolved, the People left in the Hands of another Prince, without any Reason, or any Authority, or any formed Power, to oppose him? The Government must be Administred by some body, unless we can be contented, that the Rabble should Govern.

But I shall not meddle with that Interval, between the going away of the King, and the Prince's coming to the Throne; but only cosider him as placed in the Throne, and settled there. And now we can find no alteration in the Ancient Goverment of the Nation, but only the exchange of Persons; and all things concur to make this a very advantageous and acceptable Change, excepting such difficulties, as usually accompany such Revolutions.

The *Monarchy* is the same still, and the *Three Estates* of the Nation the same; the Church of *England*, and the Laws and Liberties of the Nation secured; and no prospect of securing them by any other means: so that here is nothing to prejudice any Man against the present Government, or to make the Restoration of the dispossessed Prince necessary, as there was in the late Usurpation, but only a mistaken Notion of Allegiance to that Prince, whom we suppose to have the legal Right though he be dispossessed, and another Established in his Throne; which I have already proved to be a mistake.

But not to dispute the legal Right (which is nothing to my present purpose) here is a settled Government, which was not in the former Case.

Their present *Majesties* are in the full Possession of the Throne, and Administration of the Government by a National submission and consent; for though some Men dispute, whether a Convention of the Estates, not called by the Kings Writ be a legal Parliament,

due to Sovereign Powers, &c.

Parliament, yet all Men must confess, that they are the Representatives of the Nation; or else a Nation can have no Representatives, when it has no King in the Throne, or when there is any dispute about the Title to the Crown.

Now, though this might be improved farther, I shall content my self only to say; that the consent and submission of the Convention, especially when confirmed by subsequent Parliaments, is a National Act, and makes a Settlement of the Government, especially since the generality of the Nation have so willingly and chearfully submitted, and bound their Allegiance by Oath; which is a very different thing from submitting to mere force, when the inclination of the Nation stands bent another way; when there is nothing but mere force, it may admit some dispute, when the Government is settled; but though in some cases, it may be hard to determine, when the Government is so settled, as to make Allegiance due; this is no reason to deny Allegiance, when there is a vissible Settlement. If this be not a settled Government, I know not what is; I am sure, we have reason to pray for the continuance of it; when nothing can unsettle it, but such a Power, as will overturn our Religion and Liberties with it. It is indeed commonly said, as I observed before, that the submission of the People without the submission of the Prince, cannot transfer the Government; by which they may mean the legal Right of Government: Now to avoid unnecessary Disputes, suppose this were true; yet the submission of the People, when their Prince has left them, if it cannot give a legal Right to another Prince, yet it may give an actual Settlement to him; and that is all we are enquiring after. This I think is a sufficient answer to that odious Comparison between the late Usurpations, and this present Revolution.

I shall conclude the whole with answering an Objection, Object. which many, who refuse the Oaths, place great confidence in; and that is from the Laws of the Land: In all such cases as these, the Laws, they say, are the measure of our Duty, and the Rule of Conscience, and therefore we must own no King, but whom the Law owns to be King; that is, in an Hereditary Monarchy, the right Heir: and to pay and swear Allegiance to any other Prince, though possessed of the Throne, when the rightful King is dispossessed, or the right Heir living, is contrary to our duty to God, because contrary to the Laws of the Land.

H 2   1. In

Answ. 1. In answer to this I consider; this is no real Objection against any thing, I have said; but all that I have said, if it prove true, is a sufficient answer to this: The Laws of the Land are the Rule of Conscience, when they do not contradict the Laws of God: but when they do, they are no Rule to us; but their obligation must give place to a Divine Authority. Suppose then there were an express Law, that the Subjects of *England* should own no King, but the right Heir; and notwithstanding this Law (as it will sometimes happen, and has often happened in *England*) a Prince who is not the right Heir, should get into the Throne, and settle himself there: If the Divine Law in such a case, commands us to pay all the obedience and duty of Subjects, to a Prince in the actual Possession of the Throne, and the Law of the Land forbids it, which must we obey, the Law of God, or the Law of the Land? This, I think is no dispute; and therefore it is in vain to urge the Laws of the Land in any case, where we are under a Superior Authority: let them first prove that no King is set up by God against the Laws of the Land; and then I will confess, we must own none but legal Kings, for we must own no Kings, whom God does not make, and who have not Gods Authority.

2. The *English* Monarchy is Hereditary, and the lineal Heir has the legal Right to the Crown; grant this: but still we must consider, how far this is a Law to all private Subjects; how far every Subject is bound in Conscience by this Constitution, to give the Possession of the Crown to the right Heir, and not to suffer any one else to take it; or if he do, not to pay Allegiance to him, or own him for his King. What Law is there, that says this? And I think, the reason of the thing does not prove it. The Law does not refer the Cognizance of such matters to private Subjects; and therefore they are not by Law bound to take care of it, and I know nothing but Law can bind us to a legal Constitution. Legal Rights must be determined by a legal Authority; and there is no Authority can take Cognizance of the Titles and Claims of Princes, and the disposal of the Crown, but the *Estates* of the Realm: They indeed are obliged to take notice of the legal Descent of the Crown, and if through mistake or any other cause, they set the Crown upon a wrong Head, they must answer for it; but private Subjects, who have no legal Cognizance of the matter, are bound by no Law, that I know of, to disown a King,

a King, whom the *Estates* have owned, though they should think the Right is in another. If Authority may not over-rule private Subjects in these cases, even against their own private Opinions, and justifie their Obedience to a King, who is placed in the Throne, Subjects are in a very ill case, who have no Authority to Judge, and no Power to Resist: There are numerous cases, wherein Subjects must acquiesce in the determinations of a legal Authority against what they think a legal Right: the reason and necessities of Government require it; and the Law, which gives a Right, will not allow us to vindicate our Right against a legal Authority. And therefore it does not follow meerly from the Law of Succession, that Subjects are bound *in Conscience* to own no King, who is not the rightful Heir: And Duty and Conscience in Obedience to Laws, is the only thing I am now inquiring after.

3. Tho I have not skill enough in Law, to know certainly what our Constitution allows in this point; yet it is the declared Judgment of some of the best Lawyers of former days, and so far as I can learn, the most common and prevailing Opinion still, That our Laws do allow and require Allegiance to a King *de facto*, who is in Possession of the Throne without a legal Right. And this they have done in the Reigns of legal and rightful Kings, as my Lord *Ch. Just. Coke*, the Judges in *Bagget*'s Case, my Lord *Ch. Just. Hales*, my Lord *Ch. Just. Bridgman* in the Tryal of the Regicides, in Answer to *Cook*'s Plea; who allowed the Law, but would not allow his Case to be within the purview of it. Now when the Dispute is meerly about the Sense of the Law, to judge rightly of which, requires some skill in Law, and a great deal more than I can pretend to; Which is the safest way to resolve my Conscience? Whether to adhere to my own Judgment, against the Judgments and Opinions of the ablest Judges and Lawyers? or to rely on their Judgments (when learned Men generally agree in it) tho I do not comprehend the Reasons of their Opinions?

In moral and natural Duties, which every Man may and must understand for himself, the Case is different; we must not there rely wholly upon Authority, especially not against the Reason and Sentiments of our own Minds, tho Authority is in that Case of great use to over-rule meer Doubts and Scruples; but when the Case of Conscience is a meer Point of Law, and we conclude

clude that to be our Duty which the Law determines, I am of Opinion, That Judges and learned Lawyers, especially when they have determined the matter without any Byass on them, or any prospect of our present Affairs, are the best *Casuists*, because they understand the Law best.

That we must obey and submit to our Prince, is a Duty which the Laws of God and Nature enjoyn; and we must not suffer any Man, be he Lawyer or Divine, to perswade us, that this is not our Duty: but what Prince we must obey, and to what particular Prince we must pay our Allegiance, the Law of God does not tell us, but this we must learn from the Laws of the Land. Here is a Question then arises, Whether the Subjects of *England* (when such a Case happens) must pay their Allegiance to the King *de jure*, who is dispossessed of his Throne, or to the King *de facto*, who is possessed of it without a legal Right? Now will these Men, who ground their Dissent upon the Laws of the Land, abide by the Decision of the Law? If they will not, Why do they insist on it, and urge it, as an unanswerable Objection? If they will, Who must judge of the Sense of the Law, and from whom must they learn it? for every one is not a competent Judge of this matter, tho he thinks he very well understands the Grammatical Sense and Construction of Words. And is it not most reasonable to think that to be the Sense of the Law, which learned Judges and Lawyers have agreed is the Sense of it? Is it not reasonable to take that to be the Sense of the Law, which has been the Sense of *Westminster-Hall*, and is like to be so again, if we think fit to try it?

I do not think it so dangerous to mistake in a human Law, as in natural or divine Laws; our Obligation to obey human Laws, is that Obedience which is due to Government, and then whatever we apprehend the Sense of the Law to be, we must not pretend to obey human Laws in our Sense, in opposition to Government: if we mistake with Authority, and obey the Law in that Sense which has been allowed in all Reigns, even of the most rightful Kings, we are safe in Conscience: And he who will advance another Sense of the Law, upon confidence of his own private Judgment, and venture his Estate and Fortune, his Liberty and Life on it, I think does neither wisely for himself, nor pays that deference he pretends to Government.

But

due to Sovereign Powers, &c.

But here is an Oath concerned, and danger of Perjury, if having sworn Allegiance to K. *James* while he is living, we swear away our Allegiance from him to K. *William* and Q. *Mary*: but I suppose legal Oaths must be expounded by the Laws; and if by the Law of the Land Allegiance to K. *James* ceases, as being out of Possession, our Oath can oblige us no longer; and if by the Law of the Land we owe Allegiance to K. *William* and Q. *Mary* as in Possession of the Throne, then we may, and ought, to swear Allegiance to them: and this being a point of Law, must be decided by the proper Judges of it; for, if we keep an Oath when the Law does not allow it, and refuse an Oath when the Law requires it, we transgress the Law. And this is not the only legal Oath, wherein Men govern themselves by Judgments of Law, I am sure as much, and I think more plainly against the express Words of the Law, than can be pretended in the Oath of Allegiance; I mean the Oath of *Simony*, in which Men swear in as general Words as can be thought of, against all Bargains or Contracts, either directly or indirectly, for the obtaining such a Living, or Spiritual Preferment; and yet make no Scruple of any such Contracts, as are not adjudged *Simony* in *Westminster-Hall*, tho they seem included in those general Words. And if we will not allow it to be a safe Rule of Conscience to obey Laws, and to take legal Oaths, in that Sense which Courts of Justice, or learned Judges and Lawyers give of them, tho we must abide by their Judgments when it comes to be tryed whether we have broken or kept these Laws; Subjects are in an ill Condition both with respect to their Consciences, their Lives, and Estates.

This might very well serve in Answer to the Argument from Law; for it is acknowledged, That there is great Authority for our Allegiance to a King *de facto*, when the King *de jure* is dispossessed: but I have a mind to consider this matter a little farther.

There is a *Book* lately Printed, Entituled, *The Case of Allegiance to a King in Possession*: The learned *Author* has taken a great deal of pains in considering our Statutes and Histories; and his Design is to prove, that my *L. Ch. Just. Coke* was mistaken in his Opinion, That the Statute of *Treason* 25 *Ed*. 3. c. 2. *is to be understood of a King in Possession of the Crown and Kingdom; for if there be a King regnant in Possession, tho he be* Rex de facto, & non de jure, *yet he is* Seignior le Roy *within the Purveiw of this Statute; and the other that hath Right, and is out of Possession, is not within*

The Case of Allegiance, &c.

within the Act. It is too long a *Book* to be particularly answered here; but as I apprehend, his Fault is, that he does not reason right upon matters of Fact; and some of his fundamental Mistakes may be answered in a small compass: and I choose the rather to do it, because they are the very same Mistakes that imposed upon me for some time.

P. 6.   Our Author thinks, *It would seem a very odd Question for any to ask, touching the Laws that are made in any settled Monarchy for the Defence of the King's Person, Crown, and Dignity, who is meant by the King in those Laws? the lawful and rightful King of that Realm, or any one that gets into the Possession of the Throne, tho he be not a rightful King, but a Usurper?*

Now this seems to me no odd Question at all; for when the Law only mentions the King, and the Law-makers certainly knew that Kings without a legal Right do often ascend the Throne; if they had intended to except all such Usurpers, they should have said so: for a King *de facto*, as the Ch. Just. asserts, is *Seignior le Roy*, or King; and there is no other King but he: for King signifies that Person who has the Supreme Government in the Nation; A King *de facto* is he who actually has the Government; that is, who is actually King; a King *de jure*, as opposed to a King *de facto*, is he who of Right should have the Government, but has it not; that is, who of Right should be King, but is not: and the Statute of Treason tells us what is Treason against him who is King, not against him who should be, but is not King.

P. 8.   But he proves, this Statute can intend only a King *de jure*, because it makes it Treason to kill the King's eldest Son, to violate the Queen, or the Prince's Wife, or the King's eldest Daughter, all which, is to secure the Succession to the Crown, and therefore cannot concern an Usurper, who has no Right himself, and therefore his Heirs have no Right to Succession; and we cannot suppose that the Law should take care to secure the Succession to the Posterity of an Usurper.

But this is no Argument to me; for the Law looks upon the Crown as Hereditary, and the Change of the Person or Royal Family, does not make the Crown cease to be Hereditary; and therefore whoever has Possession of the Crown, has an hereditary Crown, and leaves it to his Heirs, as long as they can keep it; as is plain from the Example of the three *Henries*, who succeeded each other. And this is Reason enough, why the Law should

make

make no difference upon this Account between a King *de facto & de jure*.

But, *my Lord Ch. Juſt.* Coke *does not found his Gloſs upon the fundamental Conſtitution of the Realm*, tho methinks he ſhould have underſtood it as well as our Author. But what is this fundamental Conſtitution? Why, *The Regal Authority, and the Allegiance of the Subjects, is appropriated to the lawful and rightful King*. But where does he find this fundamental Conſtitution? The fundamental Conſtitution, I take to be an hereditary Monarchy; not that the Monarchy ſhould continue always in ſuch a Family; for that may fail, or may be changed by Conqueſts or Uſurpations, as has often been, and the Conſtitution continue. The moſt that can be ſaid is, that when any particular Family, by the Providence of God, and the Conſent and Submiſſion of the People, is placed in the Throne, of Right the Crown ought to deſcend to the Heir of that Family: but ſuppoſe it does not, muſt we pay Allegiance to no other Perſon, tho poſſeſſed of the Throne? Let him ſhew me that fundamental Conſtitution, for a meer Hereditary Monarchy does not prove it; and according to the Judgment of the beſt Lawyers, the Laws of the Land require the contrary, that we muſt pay our Allegiance to him who is actually King, not to him who ought to have been King, but is not. And to think to confute this by pretending the fundamental Conſtitution of an Hereditary Monarchy, is to take that for granted which ought to have been proved.

The Queſtion is not, Whether the Monarchy be Hereditary, that is agreed; but whether in an Hereditary Monarchy we muſt pay Allegiance to no Prince who is not the legal Heir, tho poſſeſſed of the Throne; This the Lawyers deny, and produce Law for it, and if there be ſuch Laws, it is certain by Law we may pay Allegiance to a King in Poſſeſſion, notwithſtanding the fundamental Conſtitution of an Hereditary Monarchy; for the Law, which makes one, allows and commands the other; and than it is an Hereditary Monarchy with this reſerve; of paying Allegiance to the King in Poſſeſſion, when the legal Heir cannot obtain his right.

And this I take to be a very wiſe Conſtitution, which ſecures the King's Right, as far as Law can do it; but if the King ſhould be deprived of his Right (which the Experience of all Ages proves he may be) does not think fit, that the Government ſhould

The Case of the Allegiance

should sink with him, and therefore makes provision for the security of the Government and of Subjects under the Regnant Prince, which the Reasons and Necessities of Government require and justifie, though there had been no Law for it.

P. 9.   3. He says, *my Lord Coke's Gloss is contrary to the constant Practice and Custom of the Realm. For if Treason by the Custom and Practice of the Realm lay only against a King in Possession of the Crown and Kingdom,* then

1. *Those only would be attainted by our Kings and Parliaments, who acted against a King in Possession.*

2. *And then certainly a King in Possession himself, cannot be guilty of Treason for what he does while in Possession against a King out of Possession.* And yet when a King *de jure* has regained his Throne, the King *de facto* and his Adherents have been attainted by Parliament for Usurping the Throne, and opposing the right of the King *de jure*.

In answer to this, I observe, 1. That this does not prove that any one Act which is Treason against a King *de jure*, is not Treason when committed against a King *de facto*; now that is enough to prove, that Allegiance is by Law due to a King *de facto*, if Treason may be committed against him : for no Treason can be committed, where no Allegiance is due.

This is confessed, that all such Acts, as are Treason against a King *de jure*, are Treason when committed against a King *de facto*, but not, say they, because Allegiance is due to him, but because they are against the Order of Government, and therefore are Treason by the presumed consent of the King *de jure*, I answer,

That such Acts are against the Order of Government, and very destructive to it, is the only Reason why they are made Treason by Law ; and this is as good a Reason why the Law should make them Treason against a King *de facto*, as against a King *de jure*; for they are equally against the Order of Government, and destructive to it, whoever be King ; and that is the only Reason why they are made Treason at all.

The presumed Consent of the King *de jure* is a very pretty notion, and serves a great many good turns ; it makes Laws, and it makes Treason, and gives Authority to the inauthoritative Acts of a King *de facto:* that is to say (or they say nothing) that the presumed Consent of a King *de jure*, invests the King *de facto*

with

due to Sovereign Powers, &c.

with his Authority; for if he have no Authority of his own, unless the presumed Consent of the King *de jure* give him Authority, it cannot make any treasonable Act done against him to be Treason; for it cannot alter the nature of things, nor make me guilty of Treason against any Person, to whom I owe no Duty and Allegiance. And if the presumed Consent of the King *de jure* invests the King *de facto* with his Authority, it must transfer the Allegiance of Subjects too; and then Subjects are as safe in Conscience, as if the King *de jure* were on the Throne; for it seems there is his Authority and Consent, though not his Person.

But this is all meer trifling; the King *de facto* has Authority, or none of his Acts of Government can have any; for that which is done by a Person, who has no Authority can have none: whence then has he this Authority, since he has no legal Right to the Throne? Not from the presumed Consent of the King *de jure*, which is great non-sense to suppose, but from the Possession of the Throne, to which the Law it self, as well as the Principles of Reason and Religion, have annexed the Authority of Government.

2. As for the Attainders of Kings *de facto* and their Adherents in Parliament, that does not prove that Subjects cannot be guilty of Treason against a King in Possession, nor that the Statute of Treason does not relate to a King in Possession: for the Statute of Treason does not relate to the disputes of Princes, but to the Order of Government; and therefore may relate to a King in Possession, though the King himself, if he be an Usurper, when ever the rightful King regains the Possession of his Throne; if he were a Subject before, may be attainted of Treason for his Usurpation.

And these things are as consistent, as it is to take care of the Government, when such Revolutions happen, and yet to discourage all illegal Usurpations.

And yet the truth is, there is no Argument to be drawn from this; for whenever there is a Competition for the Crown, there is no doubt but he that prevails, be he King *de facto* or *de jure*, will attaint his Rival and all his Adherents: Thus it was between *Edward* IV. and *Henry* VI. between *Richard* III. and *Hen.* VII. who attainted one another; and this is no proof, what the Law of the Land is, but it proves, that Parliaments have always favored the King in Possession.

3. He argues, that *if Treason lay only against the King in Possession, whether* de jure *or* no, *the Subjects must look upon themselves as*

I 2   *obliged*

obliged upon pain of High-Treason not to admit of any claim of the King de jure — and yet *Richard* Duke of *York, put in his claim to the Crown in the Parliament* 39 H. 6. and it was received and allowed by them.

But I would fain know what kind of Treason this is for a Parliament, to whom, or to none upon Earth, appeals in such Cases can be made, to receive a Claim to the Crown? a little improvement of the Argument would make it High-Treason, for any of the Courts of *Westminster-Hall* to receive a Complaint, and try and judge a Cause against the King.

If he had said, that the Law had allowed Subjects to fight for the King *de jure* against the King in Possession, this had proved his Point, that Treason does not lie only against a King in Possession; but there is no such Law as this to be found: It is Treason to fight against the King, and that, says my Lord *Coke*, is the King in Possession, without making any reserve for the defence or re-establishment of the King *de jure*, when out of Possession: For it seems the Wisdom of the Nation has not yet thought fit to make a Law to justifie Civil Wars when such a Revolution happens, with an orderly and national Submission.

An appeal to Parliament is a proper way to declare to whom of right the Crown belongs, when there is a Competition; but though such Usurpations very often occasion Civil Wars, yet the necessity of Government requires, that the Law should always be on the side of the King in Possession, and then it can never justifie any Man in fighting against him.

P. 12, 13. &c.

4. His next Argument is, that *if Treason lay only against a King in Possession, then the Law in other regards would look upon the King in Possession, as having the dignity and honor of a King*, whereas he observes 1. That *the Law, where it considers them as Usurpers, does hardly vouchsafe that the name of King;* for in the Statute 1 *Ed.* IV. *Henry* IV. is called *Henry* Earl of *Derby*, and the *Henries* are call'd *pretensed Kings, and Kings indeed, and not of right*: But he has answered this himself, that our Law allows them the name of Kings, *with regard to their having the Execution of the Kingly Office;* that is, our Laws do not allow those to be legal Kings who have no legal Title, but yet allow them to be Kings as exercising the Regal Power, and what would he have more unless our Laws should speak non-sense? And yet he should remember that *Ed.* IV. after this had as hard words from *H.* VI. Parliament as the *Henries* had from *Edward* the Fourth's.

2. He

due to Sovereign Powers, &c.

2. He observes, that *the Law does not look upon the Acts of Government done by a King in Possession, if an Usurper, as valid and authoritative in themselves*, because they have been confirmed by Subsequent Kings; and yet he himself confesses, that they had not been invalid without such a Confirmation, but *not upon account of any Authority in these Kings but upon account of the necessity of Government, and the presumed Consent of the Kings de jure excluded from their right*. But if these Kings have no Authority, I know not how their Acts should be authoritative; he ought to have said, that the necessity of Government gives Authority to such Kings and their Acts without a legal Title, and that had been Sense; but this and the presumed Consent has been considered already.

But he has made an untoward Objection against this himself, that *the Acts of Parliament made by* Hen.IV,V,VI,*were not confirmed by the Parliament* 1 Ed. IV. and yet are good Laws still; and his answer to it is very lame, that some of their Acts of Parliament are confirmed there, *viz. An Act for Founding any Abbies or Religious Houses, &c.* but this seems to be *abundans cautela*; for the same Reason, that the Universities and other Religious Foundations renew their Charters in several Princes Reigns, though confirmed by Act of Parliament; which does not suppose, that they thought their former Charters invalid, but for their greater security desire the Confirmation of the present Powers: but when all publick Acts made by Parliaments called by Kings *de facto* are receiv'd and own'd for good Laws without any new Confirmation, that is proof enough, that they thought the Authority sufficient, whereby they were made, though the King had not a legal Right.

But yet let me add, that had it been the constant and universal Practice for the Kings *de jure*,when they return'd to their Crowns, to confirm all the judicial Acts, Grants, Statutes, &c. of the Kings *de facto*, this had been evidence enough, that the Necessities of Government require, that all the Acts of Kings *de facto* should be valid; for that is the only Reason why they are confirmed by a legal Authority; because it is necessary they should be valid, and yet convenient for the discouragement of such Usurpations, that they should not be thought valid, without a legal Confirmation, but what the necessity of Government makes valid, is valid in it self without any new Confirmation; though the Reasons of State may make such a Confirmation useful.

The next thing he undertakes to answer is *Baggot*'s Case, concerning the validity of his Patent of Naturalization granted by Hen. VI.

P. 14.

P. 16.

The Case of the Allegiance.

Hen. VI. who was only King *de facto*; though it were not confirmed by the Statute 1 *Ed.* IV. This he branches out into several Particulars, and says a great deal about it, but nothing new: He always takes Sanctuary in his old Salvoes of the necessity of the Government and the presumed Consent of the King *de jure*, which have been sufficiently considered already.

All that I shall conclude from this case (which I must take as he has represented it) is this; that the necessity of Government (for both the Judges and Council understood things better than to urge the *presumed consent of the King de jure,*) gives Authority to all those Acts of a King *de facto*, which are for the Administration of Justice, and belong to Sovereign Powers; and then by the same reason, they must justifie Subjects in paying Allegiance to such Kings; for this is necessary to Government. Our Author will allow this in all cases, which are not against the Interest of the dispossessed Prince; but this is to allow nothing, for the very Possession of the Throne, and every Act of Authority the King *de facto* does, is against the Interest of the King *de jure*: But he seems all along to mistake *Gifts and Grants, to the Diminution of the Crown* (which they would not allow to stand good, when the King *de jure* returned) for all Acts against the Personal Right and Interest of the King *de jure*: But the *Diminution of the Crown*, and *the Right of the Person*, are very different things, as he will easily see, when he considers it again,

Pag. 26. As for the Statute 11. H. 7. which indemnifies Subjects in Fighting for the King in possession; he disputes very largely about it, but I can at present make only some short Remarks on what he says.

1. He observes, that it is only said in the Preamble, *not enacted in the Body of the Statute, that the Subjects shall be obliged to pay Allegiance to the King for the time being*; but whether a Preamble be Law or no, it is an Authoritative Declaration of the Law, and that is a sufficient rule for Subjects; and if 25. *Ed.* 3. concerns Kings in Possession, it is enacted there.

Pag. 27. 2. He will not allow this Preamble to be *a direct and positive Declaration* of the Law; because *the King* only says, *that he calls to remembrance his Subjects duty of Allegiance*, &c. But if the King and Parliament declare, that they remember, this is the duty of Allegiance, does not that declare their Opinion, that it is a duty

as

due to Sovereign Powers, &c.

as effectually as can be done in any other form of words; nay somewhat more, for what they remember, they declare was so before, and not made so now, merely by their Declaration; and what the Parliament supposes and takes for granted, it more effectually declares.

3dly. He says, *what is laid down in the Preamble, is expresly* Pag. 28. *false —— that it is not reasonable, but against all Laws, Reason, and good Conscience, that the Subjects going with their Sovereign Lord to Wars, any thing should lose or forfeit for doing this their true Duty and Service of Allegiance*; Now if this be false, I know not what can be true; is the contrary to it true? that it is agreeable to *Law, Reason, and good Conscience*, that Subjects should lose or forfeit any thing for Fighting for their King? But *this is meant of Fighting for an Usurper against their lawful King*. And yet here is not one word of *Usurper*, or *Lawful King*, but our *Sovereign Lord*, whom the Law requires us to own for our Sovereign; and it is against Law, Reason, and good Conscience, that Subjects should suffer for Fighting for any Prince, whatever his Title be, whom the Law owns for Sovereign at that time: That Kings and Parliaments as he urges, have attainted Subjects upon such accounts, does not prove, that it was not against Law and Reason and good Conscience to do so; and it seems *H.* 7. who had done this himself, was now convinced of it, and took care to provide it should be so no more: I am sure my Lord *Bacon* says this Law was rather *just than legal*; and therefore owned the Reason and good Conscience of it, though he demurred about the legality.

But our Author will be so liberal, as to grant, that all this Pag. 29. *were the Body of the Statute and a direct Law*; then it is plain, that Subjects might by Law Fight for the King in Possession, and their Allegiance would oblige them to it. No, he says, *it will remain to be considered, whether the Statute can be looked upon as valid and obligatory*; and he thinks it is not.

1. *Because it was made by an Usurper*, and by an Usurpers Parliament. This is a bold stroke to call *Hen.* VII. an Usurper, who had so many Titles, and no Title set up against him; and to question the Authority of a Parliament, called by the Writ of a King in Possession; and to deny the validity of Acts of Parliament made by Usurpers, when our Statute Books are full of them, and they are owned good and valid Laws.

So

64   *The Case of the Allegiance.*

Pag. 30.   So that I will not dispute with him, whether *subsequent lawful Kings* gave their consent to this Law or not, it is sufficient, they have not repealed it; but what he urges, *that it has been in effect declared null and void,* I doubt will not pass among our Lawyers to be equivalent to a repeal; for I never yet heard, that an Act of Parliament could be repealed by consequence; but let us hear, how *subsequent Kings and Parliaments* have in effect declared it null and void; and he has thought of two ways for this.

1. By their proceeding expresly contrary to the letter of this Law; *viz.* in the Attainder of the Duke of *Northumberland* in Queen *Mary*'s time, who was sent *with an Army against Q.* Mary by *order of Council and a Warrant under the Great Seal in behalf of Queen* Jane.

2. *Their laying a contrary obligation on the Consciences of Subjects;* which he proves by the Acts concerning the Succession made by *Hen.* VIII. and the Oath of Allegiance. Now I am apt to think he is mistaken in this matter, because after all this was done, my Lord *Coke,* and other great Judges and Lawyers, have taken this for a very good Law, and therefore did not think, that it was in effect declared null and void. As for the condemnation of the Duke of *Northumberland,* it was either reconcileable with this Law, or it was not; if it were, I suppose it did not *in effect declare it null and void*; if it were not, it was a Sentence against Law; and I never heard, that an Illegal Sentence did either Repeal a Law, or declare it void. As for the Acts of Succession made by *Hen.* VIII. and the Oath of Allegiance, tho some Men, if they please, may expound them so as to contradict the Statute of 11 *Hen.* VII. yet they being subsequent Laws, made without repealing that former Statute, it seems most reasonable to me, that their Sense and Interpretation should be limited by that former unrepealed Statute; for if those Kings and Parliaments had intended to lay any obligation upon Subjects, contrary to any thing enacted by that Law, they would have repealed it; for a former and unrepealed Law must limit the Interpretation of subsequent Laws, unless we will allow the Laws to contradict each other.

This is all in our Author, that strictly concerns Law; for in what follows he proceeds to dispute against the Law, from Principles of Reason and Religion, and to prove, *that it is to be looked upon in it self null and void in respect of the matter of it,* tho it were granted, *that this Statute was made by a Legal Authority, and has*

Pag. 36.

has stood ever since unrepealed. Now this is what I at first suspected, that they would not stand to the determination of the Law in this matter, and then why do they trouble themselves and the World about Law, if nothing shall pass for a good Law, which they don't like?

If our Author carefully consider what I have already discoursed, I hope he will find a satisfactory answer to all his following objections; or at least such Principles, as will enable a Man of a great deal less skill than he has to answer them all.

But tho I am in great haste to conclude, I shall stop a little to examine the two Reasons he gives to prove that Statute 11. *Hen.* VII. which indemnifies Subjects for Fighting for a King in Possession to be a void Law with respect to the Matter, though the Authority that made it be allowed good, *viz. For it either divests the Lawful King of his Right to the Crown, and gives it to the Usurper, or it still reserves his Right to him, but yet notwithstanding, orders the Subjects to obey and stand by the King in Possession:* Pag. 37. Now a very short answer will serve for this. For,

1. The Law does not deny his Legal Right to the Crown, but yet may reasonably deny him to be King, when he is out of Possession. For a King is he, who actually administers the Government with a Regal Authority; not he, who has right to do it, but is kept from his Right, such a Prince may retain the Title of King, but he has nothing else.

2. When such a Case happens, it is not so unjust or unreasonable, as to make it a void Law, *to order Subjects to obey and stand by the King in Possession:* For the King has no Right but by Law, and then the Law may determine how far his Right shall extend; and if the King himself by the advice, consent, and authority of the Estates of the Realm (considering how often such cases happen, that a Prince who has no legal Right gets Possession of the Throne, and what desolations the disputes of Princes occasion, and how impossible it is for Subjects to avoid Fighting for the King in Possession should think fit, for the security of the Government and Publick Peace, to bind the Allegiance of Subjects to the Possession of the Throne, what iniquity is there in this Law? why may not a legal Right be bounded and limited by Laws? Why may not the Supreme Authority of the Nation make the best Provision they can to preserve the Government, to secure the Lives and Fortunes, and to ease the Con-

sciences of Subjects, in such revolutions as no Right and no Laws can prevent? Since humane Governments will not always proceed in regular Methods, provisional Laws, which are exceptions from the Constitution, but necessary in such junctures, seem to me to be highly reasonable.

Thus I have fairly represented what my thoughts are about this matter, and have taken all due care, neither to impose upon my self nor others by some little fallacies, nor to provoke any sort of Men with hard words: If what I have said, do not make other Men of my mind; yet I hope it may satisfie them, that I have something to say for my self, and that it is possible, I may be an honest Man still, tho they may think me mistaken.

THE END.

BOOKS Published by the Reverend Dr. *Sherlock*, and Printed for *W. Rogers*.

AN Anſwer to a Diſcourſe Entituled, *Papiſts Proteſting againſt Proteſtant Popery*: Being a Vindication of Papiſts not Miſrepreſented by Proteſtants, and containing a Particular Examination of *Monſieur de Meaux* late Biſhop of *Condom*, his Expoſition of the Doctrine of the Church of *Rome* in the Articles of Invocation of Saints Worſhip of Images, occaſioned by that Diſcourſe, 4° 2d Edition.

An Anſwer to the Amicable Accommodation of the Differences between the Repreſenter and the Anſwerer, 4°.

A Sermon Preached at the Funeral of the Reverend *Benjamin Calamy* D. D. and late Miniſter of St *Lawrence Jury London*, *Jan.* 7. 1685, 4°.

A Vindication of ſome Proteſtant Principles of Church Unity and Catholick Communion, from the Charge of Agreement with the Church of *Rome*: In Anſwer to a late Pamphlet Entituled, *An Agreement between the Church of England and the Church of Rome evinced from the Concertation of ſome of Her Sons, with their Brethren the Diſſenters*, 4° 2d Edition.

A Preſervative againſt Popery: Being ſome plain Directions to unlearned Proteſtants how to Diſpute with Romiſh Prieſts, Firſt Part, 4° 5th Edition.

A Second Part of the *Preſervative againſt Popery*, ſhewing how contrary Popery is to the true Ends of the Chriſtian Religion, fitted for the Inſtructions of unlearned Proteſtants, 4° Second Edition.

A Vindication of both Parts of the Preſervative againſt Popery, in Anſwer to the *Cavils* of *Lewis Sabran*, Jeſuit, 4°.

A Diſcourſe concerning the *Nature, Unity and Communion of the Catholick Church*, wherein moſt of the Controverſies relating to the Church, are briefly and plainly Stated, Firſt Part, 4°.

A Sermon Preached before the Right Honorable the Lord *Mayor* and Aldermen of the City of *London* at *Guild-Hall* Chappel, on *Sunday* November the 4th, 1688, 4°.

A Practical Diſcourſe concerning Death, Fourth Edition, 8°.

A Vindication of the Doctrine of the Holy and ever Bleſſed Trinity and the Incarnation of the Son of God, occaſioned by the brief Notes on the Creed of St. *Athanaſius* and the brief Hiſtory of the *Unitarians* or *Socinians*, and containing an Anſwer to both, 4°.